THE MESSAGE *in the* BOTTLE

Advance Praise

"*The Message in the Bottle* is an inspiring tale and a triumph of spirit. Stephanie's account is ruthlessly honest, deeply insightful, and thought-provoking. She has used her hard-won wisdom to provide hope and to lay a trail of crumbs marking the way to help others break free from this devastating legacy."

– Annabel Melnyk

"I see a reader new to 'recovery' feeling an openness and space to really think; for us recovery travelers I see honest reminders to keep going! Stephanie shows the honesty with yourself that really needs to happen before you can begin to heal and truly forgive. Truth will set you free to heal, forgive, and grow."

– Tammi Fee

"Stephanie gives the reader trust in knowing more about her in a deliberate but friendly tone. I liked the appreciation of the yin and yang of things like judgment and the nonjudgmental aspects of what are very challenging problems—those of self-denial, codependency, addiction, problems with families of origin and—ultimately—leading a life of purpose and balance (and, dare I say, happiness…)."

– Jennifer Kirby

"Stephanie's openness really made me dig deep into my past. She has expressed herself in a way that I believe the everyday person can relate to. I believe many others will identify, maybe not with the same circumstances you had, but the processes you have documented can relate to anyone."

– Kathleen Herbert

"The Message in the Bottle is one of those books that allows a reader to connect into the world and life of Stephanie and at the same time, invites reflection into one's own world. Those who have felt the burden of living in an alcoholic world will connect into the memories shared in this book and have the opportunity to explore and unravel their own experience through the questions asked along the way. While not an easy topic, *The Message in the Bottle* reads with honesty and vulnerability, while providing hope to those who have experienced similar things."

– Stacey Bout

"This book will be a gift and a blessing for anyone who has grown up in an environment with substance abuse. It invites the reader to go deeper and look into their own life for similar patterns. It's real, raw, and triumphant in the end. What I love most is how Stephanie leaves you with tools to work with."

– Lise Charriere

"It is easy to fall prey to the desire for control—even more so when everything is spiraling out of control. Stephanie McAuliffe is just another person, just like you or me. The way she is unique and remarkable—and the reason why you should pick up *The Message in the Bottle*—is that she is embracing the power of letting go. Releasing the guilt and the story, instead of gripping tight with both hands. One day at a time. A work in progress. You are not alone in the chaos. Stephanie's been there too. She wants to help you step around the hole, instead of falling in again."

— **Liz Platt**

"This book gives a voice to the other side of the devastation. Alcohol destroys families, and we really only read about the struggles of the alcoholic and their downward spiral and rehabilitation, and never the innocents that get dragged along for their ride. It is their ride, and Stephanie has given a voice to the loved ones who journey with them."

— **Rebecca Webber**

"Stephanie bravely takes you on a reflective journey of her life and the challenges of loving those that suffer from alcoholism within it. It's a beautifully vulnerable story told about her journey back to peace, love, and eventual freedom; through compassion and forgiveness, and a reclamation of self—with a beautiful invitation for you to do the same."

— **Andrea Hill**

"A very insightful look into the human mind, and eventually realizing how accepting life as it is, in order to find real peace and comfort, is key. It was a profound truth about changes, dealing with emotional turmoil and adversity that face us all in different ways. An instrumental means to discover how to express yourself, to communicate honestly and find internal happiness for yourself, something that is definitely within reach for all of us."

– **Linda Beauchamp**

"*The Message in the Bottle* highlights the dysfunction that so many of us have lived with. The legacy of generations that have gone before us. The legacy of not being able to change things, therefore the dysfunction gets passed on. Stephanie has so clearly named the elephant in the room, revealed the lessons, and shown us how to halt the dysfunction from continuing beyond us. Our life traumas are events that allow for blame to be placed on others, which never resolves the trauma within ourselves. It is the personal damage and healing that we have control of. This book reveals what's necessary to make true healing happen, in us and for us. Our health and well-being is our responsibility and the only way out of our pain and dysfunction is to heal ourselves. I would highly recommend this book to anyone who has an unresolved trauma. It is a soul-soothing book."

– **Ciel Ellis**

THE MESSAGE
in the BOTTLE

Finding Hope and Peace Amidst the Chaos
of Living with an Alcoholic

Stephanie B. McAuliffe

NEW YORK

LONDON • NASHVILLE • MELBOURNE • VANCOUVER

THE MESSAGE *in the* BOTTLE
Finding Hope and Peace Amidst the Chaos of Living with an Alcoholic

Published in New York, New York, by Morgan James Publishing in partnership with Difference Press. Morgan James is a trademark of Morgan James, LLC. www.MorganJamesPublishing.com

The Morgan James Speakers Group can bring authors to your live event. For more information or to book an event visit The Morgan James Speakers Group at www.TheMorganJamesSpeakersGroup.com.

From THERE'S A HOLE IN MY SIDEWALK: THE ROMANCE OF SELF-DISCOVERY by Portia Nelson. Copyright © 1993 by Portia Nelson. Reprinted with the permission of Beyond Words/Atria, a division of Simon & Schuster, Inc. All rights reserved.

ISBN 978-1-68350-761-1 paperback
ISBN 978-1-68350-762-8 eBook
Library of Congress Control Number: 2017913986

Cover Design by:
Rachel Lopez
www.r2cdesign.com

Interior Design by:
Bonnie Bushman
The Whole Caboodle Graphic Design

In an effort to support local communities, raise awareness and funds, Morgan James Publishing donates a percentage of all book sales for the life of each book to Habitat for Humanity Peninsula and Greater Williamsburg.

Get involved today! Visit
www.MorganJamesBuilds.com

Dedication

This book is dedicated to everyone who has touched my life.
I am who I am today because you touched me
with your grace. I would not change a thing.

Table of Contents

Introduction

"Hope is like a road in the country; there
was never a road, but when many people
walk on it, the road comes into existence."
—Lin Yutang

I wrote this book so you'll know that you aren't alone in your thoughts and your struggles in dealing with the chaos of growing up with and/or living with an alcoholic.

From an early age, I thought I had to figure out everything on my own. I felt alone in my thoughts and like there wasn't anyone I could really talk to about what was going on. It was scary to think of anyone knowing what was happening in my house or the thoughts running through my head. I couldn't let people on the outside see how I had been pulled into my loved ones' craziness.

Growing up surrounded by alcohol and people affected by alcoholics, I took on traits that I thought were solely my own. I carried a heavy sense of responsibility to make sure the people around me were happy. So much of my energy was spent doing things so that my loved ones wouldn't want to drink. At times I felt like I was walking on eggshells to keep the peace.

I used to be proud of saying that I thrived in chaos. I had my fingers on the pulse of everything happening in my life, including my loved ones. That extended into my work, and I sought out difficult projects. It seemed like I was always in the midst of saving something or someone. So much time was spent on people and things rather than on doing what really made me feel good. I was trying to save people, and I was using my accomplishments as a way to feel good.

People in my family—going back for generations—didn't really talk about feelings. There are many things that I did and thought about, but I held it all within myself. Add to that the shame of the swirl of alcohol in which I was living. I ran away from the things I didn't like, including the thoughts I had about myself. I numbed myself and distracted myself from what was really going on.

It took me a while to realize how deeply growing up around alcoholics affected me and how much it set the basis for how I lived my adult life. I share some of the not-so-pretty side of that story in this book, because, if I didn't, I wouldn't be true to myself and I wouldn't be sharing a complete journey with you. It took me a while to recognize my patterns. My hope is that reading about my patterns will spark some aha moments for you.

I wrote this book to help you identify how the pieces of your puzzle fit together, and to help you recognize the chaos and insanity this disease plays in our lives, and how much time it takes up, sometimes being all-consuming.

Labels don't really matter. I called some of the drinkers in my life *functional alcoholics* rather than *alcoholics*. *Functional alcoholic* sounds so much better, but it was really just semantics. I had to come to terms with the idea that when someone's drinking was bothering me, it was bothering me. I ignored my intuition and my dislike of the drinking because I grew up with heavy drinking being the norm. The drinkers rationalized their own drinking and, in doing so, made me question my own sanity. If it was okay with them, why wasn't it okay with me?

I share my story with you so that you may begin to give a voice to yours. When we talk about what's happening in our lives—really happening, not just the Facebook façade of pretending that everything is shiny and perfect—we can work through and finally let go. It's okay to feel our feelings and get in touch with ourselves, especially when we know we're not alone. I stepped out of the craziness and found myself. I want this for you, too.

We each have a story and a unique perspective that's all our own. We are all worthy of a life that's not consumed by the madness of the (sober or not) alcoholic. This insanity may surround us, and we sometimes carry it with us without being fully aware of its effect.

My hope is that this book assists your journey to finding peace. I share it so that you don't have to search for the tools and techniques I found and used to help me on my path to a healthier, saner, happier life. Take my hand and walk with me. I wrote this book for you.

Chapter 1

A Grapefruit Grove and a Six-Pack of Beer

"The past is but the beginning of a beginning."
—H.G. Wells

I was born into a legacy of fear and dysfunction. I get it, and I've been there. In this chapter I share my story of being raised in a home where we didn't talk about our feelings, by people who each grew up in their own dysfunction.

❧

I was conceived in the back of a station wagon in a grapefruit grove during spring break. Included in the mix was a six-pack of beer and college kids doing what comes naturally. My

1

mother tried her best to hide her pregnancy, to no avail. I can only imagine that staying at home as a single mother wasn't considered an option for my mother or for her parents. In July, my parents married, and just before Christmas, I was born. Their marriage lasted six years, during which time my two brothers came into the world.

My early memories are of running around the neighborhood with little worry. We lived in a close-knit community, one of looking out for each other. There was a sense of freedom and innocence. We were well-fed, we had a roof over our heads, our own yard, and decent clothes on our backs. We were a family that did things for each other. I remember the house, the pets, the neighbors, and my best friend Susan. Yet I have few memories of my father being at home, or of my parents being together.

Some of what I share in this book about my early childhood is based on conversations with both of my parents. I have done my best to represent conversations and recollections accurately.

My parents' early years as a family weren't easy. My brother and I both had expensive orthotics. My mother was home with us and my father went to school and worked to support our family. I know I was loved. I see it in the photographs and feel in my bones. Yet there was something missing, something I yearned for during much of my life: a sense of belonging and acceptance. Somewhere along the way, I got very lost.

I have a distinct memory of taking a trip to the store with a neighborhood couple. We were often in and out of each other's houses, so joining them on a trip to the store wasn't unusual. What I remember most is their fight upon our return. The woman was in a late stage of pregnancy, and she asked her husband for help. What I focused on was her anger as they interacted. That emotion wasn't familiar, and it frightened me. We didn't raise voices in our house, nor did we show a lot of emotion.

During my mother's pregnancy with my youngest brother, she experienced a deep depression and panic attacks. Medically, she was eventually brought to a place of relief before my youngest brother was born. In the meantime, though, I took on the blame. I thought I must have done something to cause her distress. Young children believe the world revolves around them; there was so much upset, and I assumed it must have been my fault. I took on the responsibility to make thing better. I got quiet.

There were occasions when I did speak up. At six, the old man down the street inappropriately touched me and I went to my mother, looking for her to stand up for me. I wanted her to tell his daughter, who lived across the street, what he had done. My mother's response of, "We don't want to upset the neighbors" and "Walk down the other side of the street when you pass his house on your way to school from now on" instilled the sense that I didn't matter. After the incident with the old man, I dreamt I was standing at the end of the ironing board in our kitchen and the floor opened up beneath me. My world fell out from under my feet. The dream terrified me and instilled a long-lasting fear of falling.

What memories of early dreams or events have had a long-standing impact on you? How much does the idea of everything looking normal from the outside yet not feeling that way inside resonate with you?

❧

My mother instilled in all three of her children a fierce sense of independence. That may have been driven by her own sense of not having support growing up, and so wanting to make sure we knew how to take care of ourselves. One day I wanted candy, so I put my coins in my purse and walked my six-year-old self about a mile and a half down the road to the drug store. The thought of fear never entered my mind, but when I told my mother of my adventure I was told not to do it again.

There was an underlying chaos and distraction in our house. First because of the dogs we began to raise, then, after my father moved out, because of the nanny with her baby in addition to the three of us kids. That meant, for me, that there was always something else to focus on.

My feeling of uneasiness continued into my mother's second marriage, which brought me three older stepbrothers. We moved to a new house in a new town, with dogs and cats and litters of puppies and kittens. My mother had her hands full and a new marriage to focus on. In our new neighborhood, there were woods and trees to climb, and we had the freedom to run around, often being called in only for meals or at sunset. In many ways, the new house gave me many of the same feelings as our first house, although with more people and more distractions.

I'm not sure when I first heard the phrase "Children should be seen and not heard" (which dates back to 1450), yet it was something I heard often, mostly before and during cocktail parties at our house.

My grandparents often had friends over, and the bottle of rye would be front and center on the kitchen counter. At Gram's, because we were visiting, we kids were sometimes part of the conversation and hung out with the adults. Gram's crew was known as "The boozers and snoozers." They often drank until they passed out. During social events at our home, we kids were allowed to mill about for a bit, then were sent off to our rooms. We were sometimes spoken to, yet were encouraged to be quiet. I often felt invisible while in a room full of people.

I felt vaporous, except to my stepbrother. He paid attention to me, yet threatened to kill me if I told anyone what was happening between us (I share more about this later). So from third through fifth grade, I was alone with my thoughts, unsure of what was really happening, feeling incredibly alone with no one to tell things to. Fifth grade health class brought an inkling of understanding, and I told a few neighborhood friends what was happening with my stepbrother. Word got back to people at home, and then we had a crisis in the house because of me. The abuse from my stepbrother stopped for a few weeks and then, once again, I had no protection.

In my dreams, I used to take a running start, squat down and then leap into the air with all of my might. I flew above the empty buildings and streets. High above everything, removed and safe. I had this dream often. This also began my fascination with a book, *Long Ago Elf*, in which an elf flew high above everything on the back of a dragonfly. I still love the beauty and grace of dragonflies. Have you ever felt like you wanted to run or fly away? If so, when did you feel that way? And what did you ultimately do about the situation?

∂∞∕

If I was the good girl, if I did what I was told, helped around the house, got good grades and didn't make waves, then why did I always feel like everything was my fault? Even when things happened that I had nothing to do with, I felt guilty and often

I looked for blame within myself. I must have done something to cause this. I was the reason people weren't happy.

What memories do you have of taking on responsibility for things that weren't yours to take on? Did you have feelings of guilt even when you didn't do anything wrong?

∂∽∾

Gram's house was also full of tension. On one occasion, my grandfather said something nasty to me. In tears, sitting on the stairs to the second floor, Gram came to me and told me to get over it. "That's the way he is," she said. It was the first time someone verbally told me to stuff down and ignore my feelings. My feelings didn't matter. So I felt a little less.

I had a respite for two summers living with Gram after my grandfather passed away. The decision was made to get me away from my stepbrother. For me, it was a chance to relax and be a kid. Those two summers were foundational. In many ways she doted on me. I got to play dress up in old family Victorian dresses, hang out, and swim. It was while I was living with her that I watched her numb herself with alcohol on a daily basis.

When she moved in with us after those two summers, the dynamic in the house changed. In addition to her wanting to be the matriarch, there was a new focus on cocktails starting at 5:00, and alcohol became a stronger presence in the house.

One of my chores became making ice cubes after school. The water from the prior day made the cubes for that night, and new water poured set the stage for the next day. There always had to be enough ice, and lord knows it wasn't good if we ran out. Ice cubes were reserved mostly for adult beverages, so we as kids rarely got to consume them. This was a chore I came to resent and one that was often directed by my grandmother. It meant cocktails were about to start, and the evening was lost to dinner and then silence in front of the TV.

I don't want to give the impression that we never talked as a family. We often had dinner together, but I don't remember anything other than superficial conversations. Or joking about someone mixing their peas into their mashed potatoes and gravy. Few were conversations about what was going on in the world or our family.

What are your memories of your family dynamic?

❧❦

Junior high was the time that I found art and drugs and music. I could express and lose myself by creating art and enjoying the beauty of other artists. I could be present in the moment of what I was creating; and I became somewhat prolific. My father also began to work in the art industry at that time, so my exposure was greatly expanded. When I listened to music, I felt the beat and the rhythm and I could sing and hear my voice.

When I started to smoke pot, I didn't feel as numb anymore and my friends and I would laugh. I expressed myself via these things. It was easier and safer.

It was also during that time that my mother and her second husband split. There was much uncertainty around me, and losing myself in art, drugs, and music gave me a sense of peace.

Did you feel the need to protect yourself in your younger years? If so, in what ways did you express this and in what ways did you express yourself?

৵৽

I took on a deeper seriousness. I wanted to talk about real things with my friends, not gossip about TV shows. We moved to Florida after my mother's second divorce and I don't think my new friends knew what to do with me. I had already made the decision that I was going to go to college, so my studies were important and I found myself in many AP classes.

The kids I hung out with were the partiers, and they certainly didn't understand my focus. I was remembered as someone who was always stoned. The kids in the AP classes certainly didn't understand the other half of my world. So I floated. I didn't let many people close. Why start when so many people had already been in and out of my life?

I started to blossom around this time. It was just the four of us in the house and I could breathe. Until my mother got back together with her second husband. That meant my stepbrother would be back in my life, and my world fell apart. Again.

There was no option for me other than to stay put and push through it. I finished out my junior school year, when my grades went from A's to C's. I started and ended my days with one substance or another. I felt totally and completely abandoned, and I found and used every method available to kill the pain. I rejected my mother on a whole new level, and went about living my life under the same roof where I was emotionally devoid of connection.

We moved again in my senior year of high school, and I didn't do well in our new town. Still, there was one person who I became friends with who showed me a level of intimacy I had yet to know, and his gift is something I cherish to this day. My friendship with Iggy was purely platonic, and a safe haven. I didn't have to worry about someone pawing at me, and I didn't have to worry about my feelings and words being used against me.

Our friendship was kind and gentle and open, and being with Iggy shielded me from darkness. With him I shared thoughts and feelings like I had with no one before. I could just be myself, which was rare at the age of 16. During that time, I learned about light and sweet coffee which we would get on the way to school, and to cup my lit cigarette in my hand to keep it warm while I smoked. It was also the first time I trusted a man.

Our friendship was limited to the eight months I lived in that town, and it was a respite from the madness that surrounded me.

There are people who come into our lives who take and keep a special place in our hearts. They come to us sometimes at our lowest, to show us a kindness we've not known, or they see something in us that we can't see in ourselves.

I had lost my sense of worthiness and felt so incredibly alone, and Iggy was someone I could talk to. I had this feeling as well with my father's second wife. CC showed me love and attention that I hadn't felt, and she listened, at the time when I first came to the realization of what was happening with my stepbrother. Iggy and CC were two people who showed me that it was okay to open up and share my feelings, and they showed me that people were capable of doing the same. Two people in a sea of others in my life. They came and went, yet left an indelible imprint.

Do you have people in your growing years that stand out as premier in supporting you? When you were with them, how did they make you feel? Are you able to summon that feeling even if they're no longer in your life?

∂∞∂

Why did it always feel like a struggle? Why did it always feel like I had to fight for someone to hear me? How much harder did I have to try or work to be acknowledged?

In college, I was finally on my own. The dichotomy of studies and parties continued, and my father kicked my a** at the end of my freshman year when he saw my grades. My grades reflected the parties, and I got my act together after that. It was the beginning of a deeper relationship with my dad and he became a business mentor to me. I craved connection. I wanted what I had in my friendship with Iggy.

I was going to have a career and prove that I was worthy and deserving. When a professor commented to me in my junior year that I would never amount to anything, that propelled me even further. It didn't matter that I saw him the morning after a concert and wasn't in the best of conditions. I was going to prove him wrong.

Prove him wrong I did. I landed my first full-time job just out of college. I did well even though I worked for a maniac. Hans smoked three packs of cigarettes and drank about five pots of coffee a day. It was a time when we could smoke at work, and there was always a haze around his desk. He was brilliant, but rarely finished a project. Yet I felt comfortable in the familiarity of my work situation. It was chaotic and I liked it. I could make sense of the messiness, and I could fix things and make them work. What I did *mattered*.

Bill and I met the summer before senior year of college in a bar in Kenmore Square. We danced, I gave him my phone number and never expected him to call.

After college, he lived with me for the next two years when he wasn't traveling. This was a good arrangement. I could focus on my career and I didn't take a lot of time to really look at what our relationship wasn't.

I was more comfortable knowing he was there in my life, on odd weekends and in between assignments. It wasn't unlike my early years, with parallels to my parents. Bill was off building his career. Yet there was something missing, something I yearned for.

One weekend he said he had a surprise for me. I was thinking ring. He came home a day early and greeted me at the door with his dick hanging out of the front of his pants. Within a month, I had a ring on my finger. I was on the way to my own family.

He fit right into the pattern of emotionally unavailable people in my life, at arms length and with me wanting more.

৯৯৯

As you read this chapter and considered the questions, were you able to identify and pinpoint the ways some of the early events in your life had a big impact on you, and how they may still be impacting you today? Do you remember people who stood by and supported you?

Chapter 2

The Party Ended a Long Time Ago

"Even if I knew that tomorrow the world would go to pieces, I would still plant my apple tree."
—Martin Luther

I n order to not feel alone, or to not follow in the footsteps of family members, I stayed in relationships even when they weren't healthy for me. I stayed in relationships far too long. I disregarded my instincts until something major happened and I was brought to a breaking point.

෨෧

I knew it was over with Bill not long after we moved from the Boston area to New Jersey, after we'd been together for four years. It was okay when he traveled while we were in our old place, yet it didn't sit right in our new place. Was it that, or more about the digging comments he would make to "Put me in my place"?

One of the most striking moments was when he and his friend John went through all of my more than one hundred record albums. The humiliation came as they went through one by one and made comments about how the musician or band sucked or how could I have that album in my collection? I felt like I was ganged up on. I sat there quietly in my shame. Then Bill's collection. The point was the merging of our record collections as part of our "real" merge as a couple. It felt like anything but.

Bill would try to demean me with comments like "Don't embarrass me" when we went out to dinner; or with conversations after his work at the track, when all he and his friends could talk about was horseracing. When I said, "Let's talk about something else" and couldn't immediately come up with something, he would reply, "See, you have nothing to say," and would then go back to what he was comfortable with. Always about the horses or handicapping.

We moved in January. In March I knew it was over, and in May I moved out. There was no going back to Boston. I had given up my old job and an apartment I loved.

Had I really paid attention and thought more of myself, we never would have made it to the 4-year mark. But I stayed until I couldn't take it anymore. So I moved out, to a place 30 minutes south of work and an hour away from Bill. When have you stayed in a relationship long after its due date because it was comfortable, or because you didn't want to be alone?

❧

It was at that job that I met Harry. He was somewhat of a legend, as he had rebelled and walked out when one of the management consultants gave him a 15 by 15 minute schedule of work. They were trying to control him, and Harry wasn't one to be controlled. Our paths crossed once in the month we both worked there.

Fast forward a year and a half. I moved to a new job in New York City and, lo and behold, I took over Harry's code. He had consulted there for about a year before going on to another assignment. As a programmer, by working on someone's code it gives you insight into their mindset and how they think. Harry wrote good code. He thought like me, and his programs and how they tied together were easy to understand and follow.

I was at that company for two years when Harry came back for another assignment. He took over some of the work I had done and he now got to see inside of my mind and thought process. We danced around each other for about six months and found ourselves dating not long after the consultants hosted the department holiday party. I had let someone know that I liked bubbles, and Harry made sure there was plenty for the party.

Our courtship was one of hanging out, drinking and having a good time. I didn't think too much about our relationship, and was thrilled when he proposed on Christmas Eve. Our wedding reception the following October was a great party where I hired a friend to DJ and we cut the cake to a Little Feat song.

Harry was charming and chivalrous, funny, incredibly smart, and had an edge. I fell for all of these things as well as the fact that he adored me. I looked past his daily pot smoking and Crown Royal drinking. Although I had recently purchased a co-op in Brooklyn, I gave in on a move to New Jersey because he refused to move to the city.

When have you given in because, if you didn't, it probably would have meant the end of a relationship? When have you ignored your intuition and moved forward in a relationship?

❧

Two years into our marriage we bought our first house, and within two weeks of the closing I started a project that would have me in Chicago for 16 months. I would arrive home on Friday nights, exhausted from the week, and find myself unpacking and cleaning. Then back off on Sunday. It didn't take long before I felt I was coming back to a house that wasn't mine. Harry was there all week, and he liked things the way he liked them and made it known.

My full-time return home after the Chicago project was challenging. I had a long commute into the city, was managing multiple projects and teams, putting in long days, and came home from work to a bowl and/or a drink. Harry was living the life he did when we were dating, doing what he wanted, and I was there as part of the package deal. We did have fun though. On our honeymoon we bought two weeks of timeshare in Maui, which we visited two more times in our first few years. We went out to eat a few nights a week due to my schedule and not wanting to cook, and pretty much did whatever we wanted. As long as it was fun. We were what I call "irresponsibly responsible."

I worked with a young group of consultants, and while in Chicago a number of the kids were beginning to start families. Did I want children? I had said this wasn't my path many years before, yet I went through a period of deep soul searching. I wanted my own family. Yet I had already informed my mother that we wouldn't be having kids, and we had Harry's boys from a previous marriage. I asked Harry if he would stop smoking were we to try to conceive. He refused. As he said, his boys turned out OK, regardless of his smoking. I wasn't willing to take the chance. This went back and forth, like a cat and mouse game. In the end, something told me that this wasn't the time. Harry got a vasectomy.

Have you ever been in a relationship and known in your heart that it was over, yet you ignored what your instinct was telling you? Such was an incident I call Hedge Gate.

It was the summer after I returned from Chicago, I was working ungodly hours and trying to keep up with the house and gardens. My mother and her husband visited for the weekend, partly to see us and also to help me out with the house.

In the front of the house there was an enclosed porch, extending sideways to a covered porch, with connecting French doors. Harry's schedule in the morning was to sit on the couch in the enclosed porch, turn on the TV, have a cup of coffee, and smoke a bowl—not necessarily in that order. At some point during our conversation on Friday night with my mother, Harry mentioned that he loved that the rhododendrons at the end of the covered porch shielded him from the neighbors when he went out in his underwear to get the paper.

That Saturday, my mother proceeded to cut down the 10' rhododendrons to 5' nubs, fully exposing the porch. She thought it looked great, open, light and airy. Harry was off working that day and didn't see the sun shining in until Sunday morning.

To say that fumes and fireworks were coming out of his 'fro would be an understatement. Was she really trying to help me with the garden, or was this done in spite? Was she trying to break up my marriage? She always said the former, that she was trying to help, but Harry leaned to the latter, with me in between.

He left in a tornado of fury, my mother and her husband left as planned, and I had to fly back to Chicago without being able to talk with him. I was sick to my stomach and had a migraine for a week.

Given the choice between my mother or my husband, I made peace with Harry. I sucked it up. I didn't want to be divorced like my mother or my youngest brother. I was going to have my family. I didn't want to be seen as a failure.

I guess we had been married about eight years when I received a call that my great aunt (Gram's sister) had passed away. I asked my mother if she was going to come up for the service and she said no. I cried for days. Again I felt like my mother was abandoning me. I remember sitting in the living room chair and saying, "I can't do this anymore." I went to the service and was inconsolable during the repast. I felt like Betty was the last of the old ladies who had protected me, and without her I was alone.

Through a friend I found a therapist named Susan. With her, I worked through the feelings of my relationship with my mother as well as some of the challenges with Harry. We ended our sessions with me acknowledging that I knew I had to deal with his drinking—but I wasn't ready yet. Through Susan I learned about Al-Anon.

Being in that house with Harry was familiar. His patterns were pretty steady. We had his boys every other weekend, so those times centered on doing things with the boys. Their mother was quite happy that I was part of the equation since, from her perspective, at least there was one responsible adult present. Harry was known for toting an open bottle of Heineken while he drove, including when the boys were in the car. When I confronted him about it, his response was to drive with his beer poured in a cup.

We began hosting holidays at our house, and I would work for days to cook and clean and plan, making sure everything was perfect. I poured myself into his family.

I worked my a** off for holiday meals. Then one Thanksgiving, I walked into my house and there was a stranger sitting on the couch, a cousin of Harry's brother John. I had over 20 people in my house, most were sitting around watching TV or drinking and I was exhausted.

It had become an expectation that holidays would be at our house. A few weeks before the following Easter, John called and asked about Easter. My reply, "I don't know but it's not here." There was stunned silence on the other end. It was the first time I said "no" to anyone in Harry's family.

Do you find yourself taking on more than you probably should around family holidays and events, often finding yourself exhausted and not thanked or acknowledged for your efforts?

☞☜

Christmas had always been one of my favorite holidays. I took time to pick presents for friends and family and I loved the process. It was also my way of feeling that people were thinking about me. One Christmas Eve, Harry's friend Brian came to visit and the two of them proceeded to get hammered, leaving me on the sidelines.

Why did he have to get so drunk? His getting drunk meant the focus wasn't on us. When I expressed my upset at this, he turned it around on me and told me how unreasonable I was being. They were having a good time; why did I have to ruin it?

That fight was a crossroads for me. I wasn't partying like we used to, and had become more serious about my career. On the side I had started to play with making preserves, taking up most of my weekend time. I liked the creative aspect. I had fun playing with and creating my own recipes, and my friends were happy taste testers.

When I got to the point of having to quit playing with jelly or work on it full time, Harry didn't hesitate to tell me I should quit my job. I went with it, but we never really talked about what that meant financially. He was still making good money.

We continued to spend money, go out to dinner, I made preserves and each month when I paid the bills I wondered more and more where the money was going. Harry and I did finally have that conversation about money. His expectation was that my preserves business was going to bring in $5 to $10K per month, and he wasn't going to support me not "working" anymore, despite my 14-hour days.

A year and a half into Henri's Homemade (named after my grandmother, much to my mother's chagrin) and just before getting my trademark, I closed the business. I had reached another threshold and when I ran the numbers, it didn't make sense to keep going.

My and Harry's relationship continued to deteriorate, but I was going to keep it together. We rarely talked about much of anything important.

I worked my network and went back to work on Wall Street. I felt horrible and demoralized because I felt like I had no control of anything around me. As I was closing the business, Harry bought a boat.

I was back doing what I was good at, but didn't want to do. We didn't talk. We would sit on the couch many nights, him with his Crown Royal and smoking bowls, and us watching *All My Children* that he recorded each day.

Around this time I began to get interested in wine, and had a small collection of a case or two in the basement. I never liked brown liquor and hated the smell. Having a glass of wine was easy. Pop a cork, pour a glass or two and sip.

Things were easier when I sat and drank with him. Sitting and watching *All My Children*, we could focus on the show and not on what wasn't working between us.

Once he had the boat, he started to spend a night on it here and there. I didn't mind, as it gave me relief from him. I was making sure the house was clean, meals were cooked. I was back bringing in money and walking on eggshells in my own home.

Our last summer we went up to Cape Cod for a family gathering and his cousin had a female friend over. Harry and this woman were off running around, I have a feeling they were doing drugs, and the rest of the family got to watch me chase him around. They saw firsthand the insanity that we had become. They got to see how crazy and wound up I had become in trying to get him to stop.

On a fateful Tuesday in September, I was at my desk in Jersey City when a co-worker came to me and said a plane had flown into the World Trade Center. We were directly across the river and looked at the smoke billowing out of the North Tower.

Four of us standing at the window looked south and watched the second plane bank around the Statue of Liberty. The shades were down so I didn't see the impact. We ran, grabbed our things, and walked the few blocks to a co-worker's apartment.

As we sat in gridlocked traffic trying to get out of Jersey City, I looked up and saw that the South Tower was gone. There was a hole in the sky. I could tell that the North Tower wasn't going to stand, as I could see the burned out floors. It looked like matchsticks were holding up the top of the building. I turned around, looked back, and then it too was gone.

My office was closed for a few days. Then, for weeks, I looked upon the wreckage and I smelled it every day as I went to and from the office.

A month later we celebrated our tenth anniversary and went into the city. The first night was fun, we partied. The second day I went to a museum and when I tried to catch up with him, I couldn't find him. He was holed away in a bar and by the time we connected late afternoon, he was well on his way to his usual state and I was sober and not happy.

9/11, the stories, my co-workers sharing emails of watching people jump, making their own ultimate choice, made me realize that life is too short. I was approaching 40, and I didn't want to continue living in the chaos I was in. Harry and I didn't have a life. We lived under a roof together, a few nights a week.

Have you experienced a pivotal moment that made you look at your life and ask, "What the hell am I doing?" What, if any, were the signs before the event that you ignored, and how did you come to your realization?

❧❧

It was during that time that I started to go to Al-Anon meetings. I traveled to a weekly meeting a few towns away so I wouldn't be recognized. Those meetings gave me insight into how screwed up things were, and gave me strength to plan. I opened my own checking account (all of our finances were in a joint account) and had the statements mailed to me at work. I rented a storage unit and moved important files and certain pieces of art. I talked with a lawyer about my options.

Then, one day in early January, I told Harry I wanted a divorce. There was a lot of "Eff you," "You don't know what you're doing," and then accusations of scheming. End of discussion. He went drinking.

The next morning as I was dressing for work he came to me with his cup of coffee and talked about how he didn't think this was what I wanted, trying to instill doubt. When I asked him if he was willing to go to rehab, I got my answer when he picked up his coffee, walked away and closed the door.

I had often tried to talk with him about his drinking and smoking. His response was always, "I can quit anytime I want, I just don't want to." We went round and round with this so many times. The conversation depressed me and pissed him off. Then he would usually drink and smoke more out of spite. It drove us further apart.

Do you have people in your life who say the same—"I can quit anytime I want"—yet they continue in their old patterns? Does the conversation run circles in your brain because it never seems to go anywhere? How do you feel when it comes up, and how do you find yourself reacting?

☙❧

Even though I knew I was losing my job due to my company closing, we went forward with the divorce. Three weeks of negotiation resulted in a property settlement agreement, papers filed, I moved in March and the divorce was final in May.

Not long after the divorce, I stopped going to Al-Anon meetings. I was out of the house, away from Harry. I had been collecting unemployment, and not working gave me time to deal with lawyers and accountants and then time to put together my resume. I had everything under control.

When we got married and combined our households, we had a total of two TVs. Toward the end of our marriage I counted 10 TVs, three of them in the enclosed porch. Most were on almost all the time. Every time I walked into the house, there was noise from one or multiple TVs. As part of our negotiation, I took two. I heard from a friend after I was gone that at least one of them was replaced.

Harry had always been an Elvis Presley fan and I had purchased a number of CD box sets for him as gifts. One day as I was packing, he put in a CD and started playing "Are You Lonesome Tonight?" I told him it wasn't fair, and to turn it off. He did. I think he finally knew how alone I had felt for so long. We had been in a relationship together in name only. Living mostly separate lives.

Have you had or do you have a relationship where you felt alone even though you were living with the person? Where you were together physically, but not really together? Why did you, or why do you, stay?

I moved to a tight-knit neighborhood 20 minutes north, where the families welcomed me. It was just what I needed. I didn't turn on the TV or stereo for a week.

෧෧

Staying in a relationship when it's not healthy can be a way to avoid noticing other things that are going on in your life that seem even more difficult. Sometimes we ignore what's really going on because we aren't able to process it at the time. But letting it linger often increases the impact at a later date.

Chapter 3

Sometimes Love Isn't Enough

*"The beginning of love is to let
those we love be perfectly themselves."*
—Thomas Merton

I held onto an unhealthy relationship because I couldn't let go of the dream it represented for me—until holding on almost killed me because of the stress.

❦

I took a year off from dating after my divorce from Harry was final. I stopped drinking for about six months to clear my head. I finally landed a new job late July and went back to work. One year after my divorce I met Dana at a family wedding. He had

29

been a professional chef, me a foodie. We hit it off and soon after we began to correspond via email. We saw each again in September at a family BBQ and our first date was in October.

In the meantime, I learned about our family connection. His father babysat my father when they were kids. We shared first cousins, although no blood relation as my father was adopted. His was a good family, and being with him felt safe.

Our dates spanned entire weekends, me in New Jersey, he in Boston. I had no doubts about being with him, even to a friend's surprise when he proposed on Christmas Eve, three months into our courtship. I had done some soul searching the year on my own and felt like I was in a good place.

His uncle married us along the beach in April in Maine, and we cooked for 50 at our reception at his sister's house. Our reception felt like old home week. My mother hadn't seen my aunt in many years and we all got to relax and hang out.

Dana quickly moved to New Jersey, and within a month was working in the Wall Street area. Six months later we bought our house and settled in. We were both making good money and were happy in our jobs. Many evenings I came home to a nice dinner, and we would sit in the dining room, eat dinner, and share a bottle of wine over games of cribbage. I had kept the timeshares in the split from Harry, and we traveled.

The first four years were all I had dreamed of, and I poured everything into my work, home, gardens and my marriage. It seemed like we were creating something bigger than the two of us.

Yet our first Christmas in the house saw Dana with no present for me. I couldn't believe that on my favorite holiday, he had done nothing. The year before he had given me a ring.

I went to the mall with friends to get out of the house. When I described my upset to one of the women, she said, "Get over it. My husband never gets me anything." I couldn't understand how she found that acceptable. How can you live in a house with someone who is your partner and be okay with knowing they put no thought or effort into you or your relationship?

Dana would often say, "Every day is Christmas, and I show you by doing things for you all the time." Baloney. That was an excuse.

Yet I got used to not expecting anything. We stopped getting Christmas trees. In my mind I used the excuse of the mess and the cats to no longer put up a tree. I didn't want to be reminded of what wasn't.

Where have you put your feelings aside, or swallowed them? Where have you made excuses to hide the pain of not getting or doing something you want?

&∽&

Two of the main ways to commute into NYC are by train or ferry. One night there were major train delays and I told Dana I'd pick him up at the boat. After riding the ferry this once, Dana shared my love of the 40-minute boat ride into lower Manhattan. More attractive was the bar on the boat, and I now found myself coming home to him already having a few beers or cocktails.

We were no longer starting on the same playing field, and I hated coming home to the smell of alcohol on his breath. As the pressure of his job got worse he drank more. The stress was getting to him as they downsized, and he was eventually put on third shift work. We rarely saw each other except for weekends and our cohesion was lost. He was eventually let go after five years, and I blamed the stress of the job in its last year for Dana's increased drinking.

When have you found and made excuses for something a loved one was doing in order to take the focus off of them, and thus your deteriorating relationship?

❧

Five years into our marriage Dana failed his stress test, and within a few weeks went in for bypass surgery, timed so that we could keep our planned visit with my Dad in New Orleans. I was terrified when they rolled him away and spent hours each day visiting him, taking walks with him through the hospital hallways to help build his strength.

The telecom market Dana had been working in had all but dried up, so he went back to his first career as a chef. He found his way to a country club, and began working every day except Mondays and Tuesdays. I took on bigger assignments and poured myself even more into my work. He wasn't home, so why should I rush home to be in a house by myself?

This was when I had my first health scare, thinking I was having my own heart attack. It turned out to be high blood pressure. I spent a night in the hospital, and Dana's visit was brief. I lay in the bed, phone in hand, and continued to focus on my work. I had a major deadline to meet.

Where have you put the focus on external responsibilities rather than on yourself and your health? In what instances do you put more time into your achievements rather than your spiritual health?

❧

Dana's drinking got worse and he often came home half in the bag. I would lie in bed, near sleep, and that old familiar smell was there when he came in to kiss me goodnight. Somehow I convinced Dana to go to a local five-day detox program. Their process was to put you in a semi-comatose state to minimize the comedown, and then hope there was a good start for the next step of 14 days of rehab. Dana refused rehab.

He slowed down his drinking for a while and then he was right back at it. Even worse. I hated Monday and Tuesday, as I never knew what I was going to walk into when I got home. I would feel dread on the ride home and then a knot in the pit of my stomach when I turned onto our street. Many of those nights, I could hear Alice in Chains' *Unplugged* CD blasting from the speakers while still in the driveway.

There was often an attempt at dinner, yet it was rarely good. I was working my a** off, paying all of the bills, the house was clean, and I hated coming home. If I tried to talk with him about his drinking, he would respond with a snarky comeback.

I wondered what he had to be depressed about. When I walked in the living room, Dana would often be drunk, singing along and head bowed or in his hands. I hated coming home, but I loved him with all of my heart and did everything I could think of to make things perfect so he wouldn't want to drink. His therapist told him to meditate.

To keep himself busy he often started projects in the house. Or he would paint. Uneven, sloppy, unfinished. There were few rooms that didn't have the marks of a project. We built a wine room in the basement to store the growing collection that started from trips to Napa, that I continued to expand. Daily emails of wine deals consumed a lot of my free time.

Soon after my health scare, I moved to a new role at my company and shared a little of what was happening with my boss. One Friday we were working on the plans for the next 6 to 12 months and I received a text from Dana: "It's over." I thought he had been fired.

My boss questioned how I was getting any work done. She saw the chaos I was dealing with and the fear that I felt, having received multiple texts and calls that day. The work provided me something to focus on other than home. When I got home, Dana told me he had quit.

I told him to move out or go to rehab. He had no excuse to not go, and the alternative was the streets. It was my attempt to try to get some control. The next day we called a facility that came highly recommended, and in his discussion with the counselor he shared that he was drinking upwards of 18 beers each day, starting by 10am. How could I have not known this?

At least then I knew where his money and the recycling bags were going. He always drove to the recycling facility and kept everything in the back of his car, well hidden. I was floored.

When have you remained in denial instead of dealing with a situation head-on? Did that denial really keep you safe? What was the end result for you?

∂•⊱

During his first week at rehab, I was home alone through Hurricane Sandy and lived in the house for a week without heat or power. My storm within a storm. Two weeks into rehab, I attended the family education program, and the first two days were for the loved ones of the people in recovery. The following three days, we all attended together.

I got to see other couples and families who were going through many of the same things, some worse. It was during this program I learned that *I* had to recover as well, and at the end of the five days we each took a card and wrote what we were going to do going forward. "I will take in all the help and support that surrounds me." Written from my heart. Accepting help was foreign to me.

A week later I brought Dana home, after storing the booze in the neighbors' basement and locking the door to the wine room. I had hope for a new beginning. I supported him in every way imaginable, didn't drink in the house or in front of him, and the first four months were great.

I saw the man I had fallen in love with re-emerge. His eyes were bright, his complexion clear and no longer red and ruddy. He was smiling and we were generally happy. Although I was at times resentful because I felt like I couldn't fully live my life within my own house.

It often felt like he was going through the motions. I didn't know if he had quit drinking because of me and my ultimatum, or because he really wanted to. Four months out of rehab, he drank again. He stopped again for about a month, things cleared up, and I focused on helping any way I could.

Thus began a dance we would do for the following year. Me fighting harder to control his drinking and build a bubble around him, a bubble that is impossible to build.

Where are you putting off what you need to do for yourself and are instead focusing on trying to help your loved one with their drinking?

∂∽∂

I went to weekly Al-Anon meetings. I stuck with my promise and in those meetings I found people with the same thoughts and feelings that I had. I started to realize I wasn't as crazy as I thought. I also started to share in the meetings, and it was freeing to talk about some of what I was feeling. I learned that there are often relapses. My situation wasn't unique.

My trips to visit family always seemed to spark a new bout of drinking or a crisis. One probably had nothing to do with the other, other than Dana having more time than usual on his hands and I wasn't there to police him. I would come home and have a sense he'd been drinking. I could tell by the tremor in his hands. When we first met he said it was normal. It wasn't.

The visit that rocked me was a vacation with my mother, made un-enjoyable by drunken phone calls. I wasn't able to relax. He picked me up; I immediately found an empty beer can behind the passenger seat.

When I got home, I went to the computer to find an unsent email to his culinary school girlfriend, inviting her to visit any Wednesday, his day off. The draft included our home address. My therapist tried to explain it away due to the alcohol; a drunken act that didn't mean anything. A month later I went to the hospital with a second heart attack scare. Dana didn't visit during my overnight stay. I was eventually diagnosed with a hiatal hernia.

Dana's sober times became shorter and shorter, to the point where he couldn't keep it together for much more than a week. This was almost worse than him drinking all the time because now I really never knew what I was walking into when I came home.

He also started to get really weird and would text me as I was driving home. He would go to the beach and drink, and text me when he saw me drive by on my commute home. He'd sober up enough to drive home, eventually.

His drinking and driving tied me up in knots. Was he going to drive into a ditch, hit someone, get pulled over? I left Harry with almost nothing, and when I went back to work was down to my last $1,200 in the bank. I was not going to lose the house I had worked so hard for due to Dana's drinking. Yet I lay awake many nights, terrified of getting a phone call, until he came in the door. He was drunk but he was safe. I still held out hope.

Heavy drinkers often kick in their sleep. Dana was kicking a lot at night and I wasn't sleeping. I asked him to sleep elsewhere so I wasn't so wiped out when I went to work. He began to sleep in another room, and even though there was a bed available, slept on the rug. He never really did explain this, and I stopped suggesting he get more comfortable. I felt like he was trying to punish himself.

He was now rarely sober any day of the week. We had been sleeping apart for a month and one April night he was relatively sober. We sat on the couch and talked. As I curled up in bed and he came in to kiss me goodnight, I asked him to join me. He spooned me and I lay there sobbing, from deep in my belly. In my heart I knew it was the last night he was ever going to hold me. I cried through the night and woke up the same. We woke up where we started. The pain and despair was like nothing I had ever felt. I loved this man with all of my heart and was supposed to grow old with him. Yet I couldn't do it anymore. I had nothing left.

Divorce can be quick. Two months after that night I handed him the divorce settlement agreement and went to a meeting. He had moved into a sober living house about a week earlier, after landing in ICU with major internal bleeding—a combination of alcohol and antibiotics that ripped his stomach apart. We thought that was his bottom.

At the meeting, I shared that an hour earlier I had just handed my husband divorce papers. After a year and a half, many in the meeting were familiar with my story. I held it together for the first sentence of the reading, and then sobbed through the rest of the page. The reading was about pain and I cried, stopping to pull myself together enough to read a little more. It was the first time I felt like anyone had really held space for me in this way and listened without thinking about what they were going to say next and without judgment. I bared my pain and it was a safe place.

A few weeks later I received a call from my lawyer: a court date had opened up the following week. I was stunned at the quickness and then thought, *What's the difference between two weeks or two months? I'm divorcing him for a reason.* That morning I had been looking through pictures on my phone and found one of Dana passed out with a drill in his hand, laying on a piece of plywood in the dining room. The time of the picture was early evening, a few years back.

Dana had been in the sober living house for 3 weeks when we went to court. He knew protecting myself was a big motivation for the divorce. I wanted to believe there could be a chance for us if he could make it to six months of sobriety and we talked about this a lot. I was still looking for a way to make it work.

I hired him to help me with projects around the house. It was money in his pocket, and he did good work when he was sober. Yet I felt like I didn't have any privacy inside or out, so I stopped the projects.

I had started a program by Danielle LaPorte called The Desire Map, which is about defining how you want to feel in various aspects of your life and thus defining your core desired feelings. I didn't want to have to hide my notebooks from him.

As much as I wanted to trust that Dana could keep it together, I started to listen to my intuition and the feeling came to me: it's not "if" but "when." Toward the end of the year I told him of my decision and my feelings, something I had to tell him a number of times. I had changed my mind so many times before, why would he think any differently?

Where do you hold onto the dream that things will be perfect when your loved one stops drinking? Are they breaking your heart by drinking so much? I felt the same with Dana, and I so wanted him to stop. I thought it would solve everything.

෨෧

When we try to hold onto a relationship that isn't working, we can lose ourselves. The stress of the situation can make us sick. It's hard to let go of a dream, however, and when all of our energy goes into managing the gap between that dream and the reality, it's time to look deeply.

Chapter 4

How Big Can I Make This Cocoon?

*"You don't have to suffer
continual chaos in order to grow."*
—John C. Lilly

U nderstanding how you've tried to protect yourself can be hard sometimes when you're in the middle of a bad situation. Stepping back and taking an observer's viewpoint has helped me to see how I built walls around myself out of fear.

৵৽

I came across as fearless, but on the inside I was anything but. Have you found yourself putting up walls to try to protect yourself, only to have the opposite of what you wanted happen?

As young children, we enter the world full of love and curiosity. It isn't until the adults in our life impress upon us their own fears that we take on many of those same feelings. We're molded by our families, both the good and the not-so-good. And much of what our adults pass on they learned from the adults in their lives.

I didn't feel fear until I was told to. My first memories of being afraid relate to the old man down the street, except with him I was anything but fearless on the outside. Walking by his house, I felt the visceral reaction of fear run through my body. It was a reaction to what could happen again. Would he come out of the house, would he approach me again, what would I do? I had been told to stay away from him, yet I had to walk by his house to and from school, and there was no other route.

As much as I've processed this and let it go, if I try hard enough I can take myself back to that same old feeling. The deep feeling of fear and of what might happen. The adrenalin starts to flow and I verge on feelings of fight or flight. Do you remember your first situation of feeling fear, deep fear, and can you see how it shaped some of your decisions? There is no intent for judgment here, just pure observation. It is so often these early situations of fear that form a basis for what we do, without us fully realizing it. Our reactions become automatic.

৵৶

I started to build walls in an attempt to protect myself, and it often didn't get me the result I wanted. My walls kept out the healthy people. It was too much work. I ultimately let in the wrong people, those same people that played into my fears. My stepbrother being a case in point. He paid attention to me and then it became an abusive relationship. When I did realize what was happening to me, I didn't feel able to tell anyone because of his threats. What's a child to do with this? I held it in and added to the stress that had already begun to accumulate.

I didn't speak up because I was afraid of being rejected. I began to manage the negative, making decisions in order to make sure something didn't happen, rather than doing things to make things happen.

In my career, though, I was fearless. I took on bigger projects, moved to new jobs and didn't think about failure. Yet once in a job, again I was the good girl, aiming for perfection so people wouldn't find fault. It became a vicious cycle.

I kept my armor up. I powered my way through what I needed, to get what I wanted. All the while, keeping people at arm's length. This was safer. People couldn't get too close, and if they did, I usually did something to push them away.

The thought of being vulnerable with someone scared the insides out of me. Even though this was what I really wanted, I wasn't willing to fully expose myself. It was easier to keep people away. It gave me a false sense of security.

I would meet people I initially felt safe with—Bill, Harry, Dana. All three had addictive personalities, and eventually they all played into my fears. Or I should say I played into my own fears and thus made them real.

Tu quoque is a debate tactic in which a debater will attack their opponent's credibility by claiming that they're a hypocrite, and answering criticism with criticism. Bill, Harry, and Dana were all masters. Many times when I would bring things up, they would turn the argument right back around on me. It made me question my sanity and think there was something wrong with me. There are many masters of *tu quoque*, and it seems to be a trait shared amongst addictive personalities.

They weren't willing to see their own bullcrap or weren't willing to have the conversation, so turned the argument around on me. Does this sound familiar? You want to have a conversation, talk something through, and it feels like a boomerang? If this resonates, you probably just stopped bringing things up, too. Eventually it's not worth the effort, when the finger inevitably gets pointed right back at you.

∽∾

This followed the same pattern I took on with my mother. I never knew why I was afraid to bring things up with her, even something as simple as in fifth grade saying I didn't like wearing stretchy pants anymore, I wanted to wear jeans just like the other kids in school. Or in eighth grade when I wanted to start shaving my legs.

To her neither was a big deal. To me both were huge examples of expressing what I wanted. I was often afraid of and anticipated her negative reaction. I built up in my mind and felt in my body my own anxiety. Learning about her panic attacks explained so many things.

In each of my relationships, I began to gain weight when things started to go south. I appeased myself by eating and drinking.

My weight became a great source of unhappiness. I put the blame on myself. I used my layers of fat to keep them away, rather than dealing with the fear I was holding in and the fear of standing up for myself.

I let each situation get to a breaking point before doing what I needed to do for me. The negative energy continued to build in my body, and the armor grew heavier.

Once I removed myself from each relationship, I slowly lost the weight. As I shed some of the layers of stress and pain, the weight went with them. Yet I still wore my coat of armor. I always had a new reason to protect myself.

How can someone who has been so successful in their career be so tied up in knots on the inside? I was terrified to let anyone know what I was really feeling. I couldn't let anyone in on my dark secrets, I was terrified of letting anyone see me as I really was.

How could they? I had put up so many walls and swallowed so much negativity that I felt like I had to push my way through to get what I wanted. My insides and outsides were at diametrically opposite sides of the planet.

On social media, we present a likeness of ourselves that shows the world how great we are, the wonderful things we're doing, the amazing places we're going. It becomes a big game of comparison, and few people get to see our insides. How much of yourself are you hiding, and are there people in your life with whom you can really let yourself be seen?

❧

My therapists knew what had happened to me. Our sessions focused on the "what," the events in my life. That way I could point the finger. See what these people had done to me! I did talk about how these events made me feel, and then I would try to talk through things with my loved one, further fracturing the relationship.

For many years, when my mother and I did see each other, I would want to discuss our rocky past. Her reaction would often be "What do you want to deal with now?" with that tone of voice I had come to fear. I had questions and wanted to better understand. She didn't want to go into these conversations because of her own feelings about the past.

One of my most pressing questions was why she had never told me it wasn't my fault. In between Bill and Harry, my mother visited me in New Jersey. I wasn't prepared for an at home visit, so we met in a local mall (another attempt at self-protection). I asked her that question and broke out in tears when she finally said, "It wasn't your fault." It was the beginning of a thaw.

When initially asked, the question was aimed at the situation with my stepbrother. I had also blamed myself for my mother's split from my father, and that I had done something to cause the situation with the old man down the street. What had I done to deserve all this?

I now know that the question went deeper. I had somehow taken on the responsibility of my mother's panic attacks and was terrified of saying or doing something to make her upset. I had walked on eggshells in every significant relationship in my life, carrying this fear into each one, feeling like I didn't have peace where I lived. This is why I asked if you could remember your first experience with fear. Our early experiences drive so many of our future decisions and when we know how it started, we can begin to understand how to unwind it.

෧෧

I felt like I had to struggle for everything I achieved. I pushed my way through on pure power and adrenalin. I think back to my discovery of art and learning about the artist's struggle. Toiling through the years, many not making it past the fight. For me to achieve, it had to be hard. I made it so, just so I could prove to myself and others how hard I had worked. That was my achievement.

Growing up in the Episcopal church, we were taught the opposite of love is hate. I opened my heart to Bill, Harry and Dana and loved them as I could. Yet when each relationship turned south, I never felt hate toward any of them. What I felt was fear.

Bill had me questioning almost everything I thought or said, the epitome of *tu quoque*. I was tied up in knots. With Harry, I held it together because of the fear of being alone, yet I was alone in my thoughts and our relationship disintegrated long before I got up the nerve to bring up divorce. With Dana, it was the epitome of walking on eggshells around him, bringing me right back to the fear I began to feel as a child.

In December 2015, from two unrelated sources, I heard about *A Course in Miracles* (ACIM). One of the December conversations was about the hero's journey, and it was the beginning of my realization of how hard I was making it on myself. How I had made situations a struggle just to prove to myself that I could make it to the other side. Feeling that old pulse of adrenalin that had become so familiar.

ACIM is a series of daily lessons that provides guidance on thought processes, on how we think about ourselves and our relationships in our world. It is a universal spiritual practice, teaching love, peace, and forgiveness.

Have you ever taken a leap of faith, feeling in your bones that something was about to change, finally for the better? That you're ready to let go of the old way?

I began the daily ACIM lessons on the first of 2016. I was ready for a new way of looking at things. I was ready for anything that would give me relief. I was tired of fighting, and the weight of my armor was getting heavy.

The lessons seemed esoteric; nevertheless, they resonated. The early lessons were about letting go, about not being attached to things because in the grand scheme *things* are really meaningless. If I want to give significance to something, then it will be so. A book or a table can be as important as I make it. I started to change the way I thought about my world.

All upsets are equal—it's the amount of stress that you put on them that makes them big or small. I so often projected what was going to happen and made decisions based on what I was *afraid* would happen. My monkey mind would take over with all of the options and scenarios of what could happen … if. I was projecting into the future, and so often what I focused on happened because I was pointed in that direction.

I saw only the past. I focused on what had happened to me, and realized that I wasn't letting go. When I went there, the negative energy in my body came right back. I was feeling those old feelings all over again.

As many therapists I had seen over the years, as many hours I had been on the couch, I had let go of some baggage, I had come to a better level of understanding, I had come to some level of forgiveness, yet the energy was all still with me.

After studying ACIM for a while, I was determined to see things differently. To let the past go, to let the events go, to find forgiveness for the people in my life, I had to change the way I thought about them and the events in my life. I had to look beyond the specifics of the events and look at my part in each situation.

I had to look into my heart, and this scared the insides out of me. I had been closed down for so long I wasn't sure how to open up. Despite that, I continued the daily lessons and I began to let go. I saw myself begin to open and let down pieces of the old armor. I finally began to feel what I had held inside for so long.

❧❦

When we are able to peek into our past, to begin to see how we tried to protect ourselves, we can begin to see how fear of something happening drove some of our decisions. Even if we're keeping people at arm's-length, we can see that it doesn't keep the negative people away. I equate discovering these insights to taking a walk, one step at a time. It doesn't happen over night, nor does it need to. Understanding the beginning puts so many things into perspective.

Chapter 5

The Seven-Letter C Word

*"You may not control all the events that happen to you,
but you can decide not to be reduced by them."*
—Maya Angelou

Control and fear are intricately tied together. Quite often, fear has driven me to try to control something. It can be hard to rein things in when everything around us feels so out of control. The next step of pulling in the pieces of our lives so that everything aligns can be hard, too.

❦

Control is a funny word, by definition: *to exercise restraint or direction over.* To me it sounds so negative, yet we all have times when control is what we think we need.

For me, sometimes it was as simple as always holding in my stomach to give the appearance of being thinner than I was (when I started this in my teens, I weighed 90 pounds, so the thought of this now seems rather ridiculous). I think about how much energy I expended, energy that could have been better spent elsewhere.

This is a realization that came to me, as I've thought about how much I held things in because of fear and judgment. It feels so much better to let my mid-section relax now. I held in my stomach for nearly 40 years.

It was all part of how I tried to control everything around me, how people saw me, and how I wanted to appear to others. Does this sound familiar? What are your first thoughts as you read this? What are some of the small ways you try to control how people see you and what they think about you?

࿐

My first memory of trying to control my world was when my mother was divorcing again and the decision was made to move to Florida. At that point, my mantra became "I'm never getting married, I'm never having children, I'm going to college and I'll never be financially dependent on a man."

I was going to be in charge of my life, and this was my plan to control it. I didn't think of it as control as a teenager, but I didn't want to ever be in the same position as my mother. I proudly shared my mantra. Not all of this held true, however, I was keenly focused on my education and then my career.

I always had a plan, a list of what I was going to do next, and I managed my life down to the fine points. I talk with friends and family now and they tell me how focused and driven I was. This I knew, yet I don't think I ever realized just how wound up I was. Everything was always in line. I knew where things were and where I was going. I had a tight grip on my life.

With both Harry and Dana, they gladly handed things over to me. Neither was diligent about paying their bills and I had always been on time and paid off loans early. In both cases, I took over paying their bills not long after we married. They were happy to hand this over to me, it was one less thing for them to think about.

They say, "To get a job done well you have to do it yourself." But all this did was put the burden on me and give them more free time. I didn't see it this way. The bills were paid and I had them under control.

I also took on the garden, much of the house cleaning and chores, food shopping. It played into the old story of the wife maintaining the house and the husband bringing home the bacon. Except I was the one bringing home the bacon, too.

Neither Dana nor Harry really cared about the dust or the bills or the gardens, and both would have been happy with macaroni and cheese most nights. I was the one setting the standards and so, to maintain them, I took on the responsibility. All in the effort to make things look good. And by making things look good, I felt good.

In many ways though, as I took on more duties, it was like trying to grip water. The tighter I tried to hold on, the faster the water flowed out of my hands.

I took great pride in my work, the projects I accomplished and how I presented myself to my world, personally and professionally. Project management fit quite well into this, as projects had to be in by a certain time, of certain quality and within a certain budget. My creative side got to come out and play as well, via the application and technical designs in my projects.

But the big thing was that I managed my projects very closely and made sure my team had everything they needed to get their work done. In many ways, I wrapped a bubble around them, just like I did with my husbands. I gave them everything they needed to do what they did. The big difference is that my teams didn't focus on drinking. And they appreciated that I cleared the way so they could focus on their work.

For years I used to proudly proclaim that I thrived in chaos. I was given the tough projects, the ones that were about to fail, the impossible deadlines—and I made many of them work. I pushed my way through, had my fingers in the dam and got everything under control. Instead of letting someone else fail and take their own responsibility, I added to my burden because if our projects were associated and you failed, then I saw *myself* as a failure. I took it all on in my attempt to make sure nothing tied to me ever failed. At times I felt like I was spinning like a top, on the verge of spinning off the table.

Have you ever found yourself wrapping yourself tightly around something or someone, thinking you were protecting them when, in actuality, you were really tying yourself up?

ॐॐ

I hit my personal bottom all at once. Convergence from all sides.

The business area I worked in went through reorganizations every six months or so, and I found myself working with my third business partner in as many years. Plans that had been put in place weren't her priority and she didn't want me there working with her.

She was another person who wanted just as much, if not more, control than I did, and she didn't care about the plans that were already in place, nor did she care about project management. She had little respect for my team or the work we did. I was the program manager but there was minimal support from senior management. She had her own plans. She brought in high priced consultants who she controlled.

Add to this the stress at home with Dana's drinking and the email to his ex. Home was no good. Work was no good. I was working crazy hours in an attempt to keep up, and still overloaded myself at home. I was trying to control everything around me due to the fear I felt, and I was always looking over my shoulder.

Not even the diagnosis of a hiatal hernia stopped me. How could I not see? I was so buried in trying to keep it together that I just started to take a pill for my stomach to kill the pain.

I have a friend who grew up with alcoholism and lives with someone who likes the bottle. Her pain is experienced as migraines. Mine went to many places in my body, but the overwhelming feeling I get is the adrenalin streaming through the center of my body.

Can you take a few moments to step away from where you are now, and look at where you feel like you have your fist tightly clenched around something? Don't think too much about it. Where does the control in your body go and how do you feel it?

❧

It's not easy to let go of something we don't see at first. When I was in the midst of saving another project or trying to make everything perfect so that either of my husbands wouldn't want to drink, I didn't see it.

My hope for you is that you start to have an inkling of where you may be on the control spectrum. For you to be able to step outside of your mind for a few minutes, and listen to your heart and intuition.

I ignored my intuition for many years and ran my life on the adrenalin I became addicted to. It made me feel alive. When I finally stepped away, I was able to see the bigger picture.

ॐॐ

I've often heard that we have everything we need. Yet when I was being driven by my "need for speed," my mind was too noisy to listen to my heart. So I started to get quiet and listen. I began to let go. When I loosened my grip, the adrenalin slowed down and my mind quieted.

Some of letting go was driven by necessity. At work there were rumors of major layoffs. My business partner had left the company and the program came to its natural conclusion. I was looking for other roles and came as close as being someone's second choice.

The following month I was one of hundreds who was laid off. I had been on the other side, one of the people left after the cuts, and the constant stress of not knowing when the axe was going to fall was awful. In retrospect, not unlike how I lived a lot of my life. Trying to control the fear of what might happen.

This was also the case with Dana. I wanted to find a way to trust him and make it work between us. We talked a lot about him being sober for six months before I could reconsider "us." I dangled the carrot in the attempt to put my own guidelines around our relationship.

After a few months, my intuition told me it wasn't a question of "if" but "when." Always wondering when he was going to drink again, not knowing what I was going to walk into on a daily basis wasn't a situation I was willing to put myself in again.

Some might call this control, and in a sense it was. I also call it establishing a healthy boundary. I was finally listening to my intuition and doing what I needed to do for myself, rather then chasing someone else's energy. When I was chasing someone or something, they were what had the real control—I had none.

❧

My focus and drive haven't gone away. They will always be with me. Yet I now know that the only person I can control is myself. There's a saying that if you say something once, you're sharing your opinion. When you say the same thing a second, third, fourth time, you're trying to control the situation.

Think back in the past week or month. Is there a situation where this happened to you? If it was you who was repeating, did it get the result you wanted? If you were on the receiving end, how did it make you feel? Unheard? Manipulated? Did you do what the person asked just to get them off of your back?

⇛⇜

Can you remember the first time you felt out of control? What was the situation? Was the feeling due to something you or someone else had done? How did you react? Did you try to rein things in or let them go? How successful were you?

⇛⇜

In your life right now, can you name one thing that you're trying to control? Is it working? Is the situation really within your control? What would happen if you completely let go?

⇛⇜

By trying to control Harry's and Dana's drinking, I was playing the role of their director, and it's no surprise now that they rebelled. For a while they appeased me in one way or another. Ultimately they gave me the middle finger, just like I would have done to me.

Why did I think I had any right to control them when I myself don't like to be controlled? My attempts were due to the fear I felt, and trying to wrap my arms around the situation in order to feel safe.

❦

When we start to put the pieces together, we are able to see how control is so often driven from a deep sense of fear, and that control and fear often create an unhealthy symbiotic relationship. It takes going back and pulling memories from our childhood to see how they play out in the decisions we make now as adults.

Chapter 6

Do You Like What I'm Doing?

*"Even if the most important person in your world rejects
you, you are still real, and you are still okay."*
—Melody Beattie

We lose our true selves when we look to external factors to prove our worth. By working and striving for the next big thing and for perfection, we sometimes give away our power, often without realizing it.

❧❦

So much of what I did, how I felt and how I reacted were intricately wound together. To feel good I had to prove myself, and to do that I felt I had to work as hard as I could on

64

everything I did. By being the good girl I removed myself from the equation of feeling how I wanted to feel. In these next pages we'll go deeper into the maze, to show you how much I gave away, and how to begin to step into your own power.

Think of a time when you put your heart and soul into something and then put it in front of someone for their reaction. Not just a reaction, but, hopefully, their approval. In that moment, waiting for their reaction, how did you feel? Tall? Proud? Small? Anxious? Quite often all four of those emotions ran through me simultaneously. Especially with things related to work or home.

At work, I strove for perfection. I ran on the adrenalin of bringing a project to completion (tall, proud) and then waited for someone to find a flaw or a mistake (small, anxious). I pushed for the 100%. A VP once told me that there's a bug in every program, and I was going to prove him wrong.

I didn't understand other people's *laissez-faire* attitude when issues did arise. Because of my overwhelming sense of responsibility, I was determined to get it right as fast as possible.

In my mind, I had to measure up to a level of perfection in order to be seen in a good light in people's eyes. When I did make a mistake, I took on something bigger, to prove myself.

The house was well kept. The inside was clean, well furnished. We ate well. It was devoid of much emotion. The outside, however, was beautiful. The gardens almost always had something in bloom. The flower beds took up more and more of the yard. When you walked by and commented on the flowers, I felt a great sense of pride.

I do love the beauty of my gardens. It's something that's passed down from my grandmother and mother. Working in my gardens didn't give the same adrenalin rush as working on projects, yet I found more and more of my free time being spent here. I could look at the beauty of what I had created with Mother Nature, and it made me feel good.

Looking good on the outside included dressing for work. By putting on a nice suit, skirt or dress, I was attempting to control how people saw me. By focusing on the outside and my ever increasing work projects, I didn't have time to look at my inside. So much of what made me feel good had little to do with how I felt about myself. I had been so numb for so long that I didn't know any other way.

What I wanted was approval. By focusing all of my attention on the reaction I received, I was giving away my power. I left my feelings in the hands of the person I was with.

As that little girl who wanted to make everything smooth, quiet, and peaceful in my family's home. As the teenager who pushed her way through high school and college to make sure she had her education and degrees. As the adult, proving herself in her profession. As a wife and girlfriend, waiting to be loved the way I wanted to be loved.

In all of these areas, I kept reaching out for more and more. In some cases, I would achieve what I sought, mostly at school and work. In my relationships, I would reach out and sometimes the other person would give a little. So I would reach some more, and keep reaching out. I was looking for something from people who weren't capable.

For yourself, take a look at your home, work, and relationships. In each of the areas, try to identify where you may be looking for approval or something else to fulfill a need. In what ways can you satisfy that need yourself? In what ways can you make subtle shifts to take back your power?

∂∽∂

All of this made me incredibly exhausted. What more could I do? How could I make it better? How could I make you feel better? I wound myself up running after all of my achievements that I often got sick.

Sickness is often a way that our body tells us to slow down. However, when I got sick, I either powered my way through it or focused on all of the things that weren't getting done and how much I had to do once I was better. There was a period where I was having monthly afflictions and dammit, I didn't have time to be sick. There was stuff to do and only I could do it.

How do you unwind the ever-growing list of things to do? It's incredible that I kept finding new things I wanted to do, read, plant, organize. The list was never ending. By adding to it, I continued to put my value in the things I did rather than how I felt.

On one of my initial Desire Map calls with a coach, we were asked how we wanted to feel. I felt a shockwave run through me because I couldn't answer. Feeling so out of touch made me afraid. But it wasn't that old adrenalin fear that used to run through me. This felt different, and I started to pay attention. In everything I did, I started to ask myself how I *wanted* to feel. Ever so slowly.

I put together a stop-doing list. It started as a list of all of the things that were forever swirling through my mind and taking up any extra energy.

When I put together my first list it was eye-opening. No wonder I never felt like I had any time! Very few of the things were actually being done for me. Yes, I liked a clean house, a good meal, and the nice gardens, but I didn't have to always be doing more.

A little dust was OK, leftovers and scrambled eggs taste really good for dinner, and did I have to plant as many things as I did in the garden, just to have to maintain them? What could I let go of? It started with looking at each item and seeing how I felt when I thought of each. If it didn't feel good, it got crossed off.

Put together a list of all the things you do daily, weekly, monthly. Once the list is compiled, do you feel better just getting it out of your head and onto paper? Now that you have the list, look at each item and identify whether they feel necessary or like an obligation. Which items make you feel good? What one thing can you stop doing right now to lighten your load? Are you doing any of these to get something from someone?

❧❧

I found my friendships changing as I began to change. I was looking at things differently. I became active in a local bicycling club and met Laura on one of the weekly rides. We became fast friends, and it was good to ride with someone on the same level that I felt like I could talk with.

She saw some of what I was going through with Dana and she got it. Her ex-husband was an alcoholic. Yet, as I started to get healthier, I saw that she blamed much of her unhappiness on him and still held that old energy from when he left her, over 12 years prior. She wasn't taking responsibility for her part of the situation. Had I been doing the same?

Laura began dating Juan, and very quickly it became apparent that it was a one-sided relationship. He rarely took her out, didn't introduce her as his girlfriend, and she was at his house a few nights a week. She often complained that he would have dating sites up on his computer. She never said anything to him, yet she came to me and repeatedly said, "I don't know what this relationship with him is." This went on for many months. She talked about being able to play games as well as him.

This made me look at things in new ways. When had I not stood up for myself in order to try to get a piece of what I wanted? How long did I stay in situations where I was unhappy, just to get a glimpse of the love and approval I sought?

Laura didn't like when I said, "Why does it have to be a game?" or "Have a conversation with him about it." She seemed more attached to the old feelings, just like I had been for years. Our friendship ended.

I was finally doing what I needed to do for me, and some people weren't comfortable with the new me. Some of these friendships were hard to let go of. And it wasn't always easy for me to make new friends. Yet I now knew that I didn't want to keep getting beat up or having the same old negative conversations that just brought up the same old negative energy and feelings.

What relationships do you feel like you're in out of a sense of obligation? What friendships feel like they've passed their logical end, yet you're both still there? People naturally come and go in our lives. Where are you holding out in hopes of getting a need fulfilled? Where are you ignoring your feelings in hopes of someone doing something for you?

৵৽

People very quickly tell us who they are, and I was now paying attention. People who I would have gravitated to in the past either didn't get past the first or second date, or we simply remained acquaintances. I was finally putting up healthy boundaries and not giving my power away so quickly.

I stopped trying to fix people or get them to like me by doing things for them. Letting go of the old patterns and ways of relating wasn't easy at first. I was so used to always giving, but in the attempt to get something back—most often acknowledgment. My friendships are now based on mutual respect and doing things with no expectations of receiving in return. It's quite freeing to just be able to be me.

৵৽

When we put our focus on gaining approval for the things we do and on striving for the next bigger thing, we often lose ourselves to those very things. When we strive to prove ourselves by our outside appearance, it's often our insides that need some TLC.

Chapter 7

How Far Down Can I Bury You?

"The loneliest moment in someone's life is when they are watching their whole world fall apart, and all they can do is stare blankly."
—F. Scott Fitzgerald

B y not dealing with the emotions in my life, they had nowhere to go but inside, often resulting in illness. By building trust in my body's wisdom, I learned how to move toward health, both mentally and physically.

❧

The stomach aches and sore throats started at an early age. If you can't express what you're feeling, or say what you need to say, or ask for what you need, where does the energy go? For some it's externalized and expressed as anger. For me, I went inside.

I remember the recurring tonsillitis, the closing of my throat. I didn't feel like I had a voice. Who was there to listen anyway? Why repeat the past by speaking up and being ignored? It was easier to swallow my feelings. Right into my stomach. The stomach aches came after the sore throats, or at least I remember that as the order. With my stomach, there wasn't anything identifiable by the doctor. Nevertheless, I felt dirty inside.

It's funny that in junior high school when many of my friends became enamored with alcohol, I wasn't. I was allowed to sit with the adults on the weekend and have a beer, so there wasn't a big draw for me.

Pot was another story. It was the mid-70's, and there was plenty to go around. My neighbor across the street loaned me her pipe and showed my friend Jean and I how to smoke, holding the smoke in our lungs for optimal effect. I loved the feeling of lightness flowing through my body. Even more so with the prescriptions filled for the adults for their dental work.

I remember my grandmother mentioning how stoned she felt when she took one of her pills. Although the situation with my stepbrother had stopped, we were still living under the same roof together, and the pills became my way to not feel the anguish as I realized what truly had happened over the course of those four years. My grandmother was a prime example of numbing pain, and I followed in her footsteps.

I became attracted to new substances as my world expanded with our move to Florida. Down there the pot was cheap, and many mornings you would see a number of teenagers smoking in the parking lot before school. The same with my senior year back in Massachusetts. I would find a substance I liked and do a lot of it until I had a bad experience with it. Then I would move on to another.

In Florida, my drug use didn't get really heavy until I found out we were moving again. I think the best way to describe it is thrashing, which continued through my senior year. Then I fell into a crowd that introduced me to mescaline and crystal meth. Laughter and speed. They made me forget about what I didn't want to think about and what I couldn't deal with. Then Quaaludes and cocaine in college.

I started to drink more when I decreased my drug use, partially out of necessity. I started to break out in hives whenever I did coke. It could have been because of what it was cut with, or my body just saying, "Enough!" There are many drugs I never tried, one being heroin. I had the opportunity and said no. Spirit must have been looking out for me that day, knowing my own tendencies.

Alcohol is so much easier. It's *everywhere*. You have to work to not be around it. With Harry and Dana, it was easy and provided an immediate and direct connection. They weren't dealing with their demons either, so we made a great team.

Once I went to work, I didn't need drugs anymore: the stress was as good as speed to me. Putting undue pressure on myself. It made me feel alive. Then after a tough week at work, I relaxed over a cocktail or two or three.

In not being able to process my emotions at the time, I focused on the events. It's a crazy circle. By focusing on the event, it brought up the old feelings of hurt and abandonment, and made me feel justified to point the finger and say, "Look what you did to me. Look how you're making me feel."

I realized that I had been playing the victim, and I played it well. "Look at how hard I'm working, can't you see what I'm doing for you, don't you appreciate what I'm doing, why can't you hear me, don't you get it?" The mental chatter was unceasing and the energy coursed through my veins.

It was easier to repeat the old stories. They justified my feelings. I wanted to prove how badly people treated me. This was easier than recognizing the feelings I didn't want to feel and easier than looking at my part in the equation.

How do you want to feel? How do you want to feel on a day to day basis? How do you want to feel when you wake up in the morning? When you to go sleep at night? How do you want to feel? Not based on someone else's needs or desires. Not based on what you did. Not based on what someone else thinks of you. How do *you* want to feel?

I don't remember how I found Danielle LaPorte, the author of The Desire Map. At this point, I don't think that matters. I just remember getting an email about the new Desire Map beta program workshops being given by selected coaches. Many of them were weekend intensives, one was an online 8-week program. This felt better to me. It gave me time to think and explore. I like to ponder and have rarely been one with a quick retort.

I knew I wanted something different. I knew there was something better for me. I took the plunge. I was stunned on that first group call when Sandi, our coach, asked that fateful question: "How do you want to feel?" I was rocked. I realized that I couldn't really answer the question.

I had turned off my feelings and numbed the pain for so long, that I didn't know how I wanted to feel. My focus had been on work, my husbands, the house—everything but me. I started to realize that while I fed myself, dressed well and had some form of exercise schedule, I wasn't feeding my soul. I had ignored her and put her on the back burner. In what ways are you not making yourself your number one priority?

∂⌒∽

My health showed me how much I wasn't dealing with my feelings. Getting sick most winters just after Christmas. Stomach aches which eventually resulted in a hiatal hernia. Two heart attack scares, the first resulting in a high blood pressure diagnosis. Sore throats even through adulthood, symbolic of feeling emotionally unable to speak. The grinding of my teeth and clenching of my jaw for all the times I didn't speak up and the stress I was feeling.

At what point was I going to finally let go of the old stories and the old energy? The energy that I had become so accustomed to, in many ways addicted to. Although it didn't make me feel good, it was familiar. It put me back in the mode of feeling inferiorly superior.

How has stress manifested itself in your body? Are you able to tie what ails you mentally to what ails you physically?

❧

I started to see the connections when one day I read an article about blood pressure medication, and how certain types of high blood pressure may be attributable to childhood trauma. This was the case with the beta blockers I was taking. My doctor and I were trying to find another medicine that wouldn't tie me to two meals a day. We tried other drugs but none worked as effectively. The research was fascinating to me.

Every time I told one of the old stories, every time I felt justified to point the finger, every time I took on that broken project, that old energy was pulsing through my veins. Because I let little out, it continued to build until it put me in the hospital. To cure it, or at least manage it, it was easier to take a pill instead of looking at *why* I was in the hospital in the first place. The mental effects had taken their toll physically.

The same for my hiatal hernia. It was easier to take a PPI (proton pump inhibitor) for heartburn every morning. At the point of that diagnosis, I don't know that I had the capacity to do anything other than take the PPI. It was near the height of the insanity with Dana.

Sometimes we have to pick the battles we want to fight. At work I had stopped fighting. The battles with my business partner weren't worth it and I stopped taking her bait. At home I still had fight left in me, and that became my focus.

The Desire Map program had a private Facebook group. I had never been on Facebook. I didn't want anyone to see my personal life. In that group, I was able to share little bits at a time and there was no judgment. I started to feel safe in exploring and sharing my feelings. I wasn't alone in my thoughts anymore.

At the end of The Desire Map group, Sandi introduced her new 100 Day Promise program. I liked the idea of 100 days of daily prompts, of exploring where each day would take me. It further deepened the connection to how I wanted to feel.

I had been letting my life pass by me. I participated, but how much was I really living? And how much was I living for me, rather than the things outside of me that I thought would make me feel good? I knew I wanted to feel differently. I was ready to change.

What are you doing for yourself daily that is just for you, for your body, mind and spirit? It doesn't have to be big or scheduled. Sometimes it can be as simple as thanking yourself for your awareness.

෧൳

Based on your observations from earlier chapters, how did you deal with the emotions you didn't feel you could express? In not wanting to or not being able to deal with a situation, how did you process those emotions: working out, eating, drugs, alcohol, sex, or just trying to ignore them? How long did this last, or does it still continue?

෧൳

How often do you replay events in your mind? When you do, what are the feelings in your body?

I often resisted feeling them because they scared me. Yet by not feeling them they controlled me. I had to feel them, one at a time, to walk through the wall of resistance. Once I did, they no longer had a hold over me.

কৈ৺ৎ

The body can begin to find relief and to release the physical ailment when we recognize the ties between body, mind, and spirit, and when we realize that what we do and don't do, what we think and what we feel manifests in the body.

Chapter 8

The Apple Doesn't Fall
Far from the Tree

"A person is what he or she thinks about all day long."
—Ralph Waldo Emerson

Despite what we want, the people we attract into our lives are often reflections of how we feel. But every day is a new day, an opportunity to begin anew and to let go of what no longer serves us.

❧

Seeing people as they are, rather than how I wanted them to be was a hard lesson for me to learn. I wanted people to be a certain way with me, yet I wasn't able to do the same.

I had unreasonable expectations for many of the people in my life and created my own unhappiness within those relationships. Talk about a never-ending cycle of failure.

I've been amazed at the number of people who have come and gone in my life who also have addictive personalities. With everything available in the world for us to latch onto, I know very few people who don't attract one thing or another. I seem to attract addictive personalities.

As I scan my life, it's the people in high school and college who also couldn't or didn't yet realize the depth of what drove them to drugs and alcohol. Bill with the gambling. Harry with the alcohol and drugs. Dana with the alcohol. The people I worked with who also thrived in chaos. Me with much of the above.

Call it the Law of Attraction, call it being comfortable with like-minded people, call it karma. It all boils down to something deep inside of us that draws similar people together.

There are certain situations that are hard to draw this conclusion with. The old man down the street, the situation with my stepbrother. It's hard to say that a six or eight-year-old could attract things that should happen to no person, ever.

Yet I think all of these experiences tie into a larger lesson. They were the beginning of a path that led me to finally healing. To finally standing in my own space and taking back my power. To finally cutting the cords to the old stories I told myself for years that kept me in my old small space, feeling unworthy and totally codependent.

If you don't ever think there will be the right job, the right partner, enough money, it becomes true. My thoughts centered around a scarcity mentality and when I focused on never having enough, I never did.

In many ways, I was just as crazy as the people around me. Yet I didn't see it until I stepped away and began to look at things objectively. I removed the emotion and began to see how I fit into all of it.

I thought I had moved past the "what" but until I really looked at the "why" and understood why I did what I did, or why the people in my life did what they did, the old stories remained. They weren't truly let go of, and the energetic cord remained.

Can you pick one of your old stories, step out of the emotions of it and look at it objectively? Can you see why the other person did what they did?

You don't have to like what happened, but in order to move past it, you have to come to a place of acceptance. Just remember that acceptance does not equal agreement.

❧

I've wavered back and forth between using the labels of "alcoholic" and "functional alcoholic" for my loved ones. But does it really matter what it's called if someone's drinking is driving us crazy? We can put labels on anything we want; however, when something is driving us crazy, it's worth a further look. Is it because someone isn't doing something we want, or not doing what we want them to do?

Knowing there's little to nothing we can do to change another person, I had to look at my reaction and how I wanted to change that. There were so many times where I tried to talk with Harry and Dana about their drinking, particularly when they were drinking. Effective? No.

I was trying to form them as I wanted them to be, not fully seeing them as they were. With both I attached the label of alcoholic, and that became the primary way I saw them.

With Dana I was finally able to separate the person from the disease and was able to recognize his struggle. My perspective toward others began to soften as I recognized the ways I had been pointing fingers and making accusations.

In what ways are you reacting to your situation and feeling like you're getting nowhere? Is it because of your expectations? Is there a way you can change your thinking, ease your expectations, and thus ease your mind?

❧❧

I don't know that I put a particular label on my mother; still, I began to see her differently. When I pointed the finger at her, blamed her for much of my travails, she reacted as any other person would have. Each time I brought up old situations, I wanted her to acknowledge what had happened. I also subconsciously wanted her to feel as much pain as I was feeling and she pushed back on having the discussions because it was too painful for her to go there.

Through those years of my early adulthood, I didn't know any other way, because I was focusing on the "what." I didn't like that my mother and my father were divorced. I didn't like going to three high schools and feeling like I had no roots. Yet she was trying to find her way as well.

To think that I was ever going to get a positive response from my mother when I was pointing the finger at her is insane. By pointing your finger at a person or situation, what are you not seeing in yourself?

☙❦

Going to the weekly Al-Anon meetings, I heard people's stories and began to realize that I wasn't the only one with craziness in my life. The things the alcoholics in our life do, the thoughts in my head, the things I did to try to get them to stop drinking. I wasn't alone in my thoughts or actions and I began to see how much of an impact alcohol had had on my life and how deep the roots go. How deep my codependence went.

The definition of insanity is doing the same thing over and over and expecting a different outcome. I used to joke that I stopped trying to read minds when I divorced Harry. Yet I didn't really communicate with him either. My expectations were askew.

I began to see my patterns and why I kept doing the same thing over and over and over again. That in thinking I had everything under control, and not listening to my heart or intuition, I was bound to repeat the same patterns. Until I took a deep and hard look at myself, I was bound to continue to repeat the past.

Looking at the "why" without labels and letting go of the judgment has been like peeling off many layers of an onion. It didn't happen overnight, but neither did my past. The stories built on each other over time. The insanity of the life I was living came to a head, and I had to make the choice to finally save myself.

In what ways are you ignoring what your heart is telling you?

∂∽∮

There is a phrase—detachment with love. We can still love a person and not like what they're doing. Instead of trying to change them, we can walk away and work to emotionally remove ourselves from their energy. I did this physically with

Harry by divorcing him. I wasn't aware of the phrase at the time and had to extricate myself. He was never going to change, so I did what I knew to be best for me.

With Dana, it came to the same result, yet I saw him from my heart. My responses were different. I had grown to the point of not picking the fight, not taking on the negative energy and of beginning to say what I needed from a place of calm.

In what ways are you afraid to speak up to a friend or loved one? By not speaking up, what part of yourself are you losing?

❧

This place of speaking my truth found its way into my friendships as well. When we change, we sometimes discover that our friends are comfortable with our old selves, but not our new selves. Friendships ended when I wasn't sitting on the barstool next to them anymore. Others ended as I began to say what I needed and to set healthy boundaries.

I made the decision and shared it with friends that I didn't want to gossip anymore. To me, going back to the same old stories brought the negative energy back through my core, and I didn't want to keep going there. Not everyone was happy with this.

When I point a finger, three are pointing back at me. How much was I judging people and not seeing and accepting them as they were, where they were?

I had continued to have expectations for people that I really had no business having. I had judged myself for years, so this just became a way of being. We're taught to compare and it's inherent in our culture. Judgment falls right in there with comparison.

When I can point a finger at something in somebody else that I don't like, it's usually really shining a light on something within myself that I don't like. Sometimes the flashlight was really bright.

Think of a situation where you have expectations. Are they realistic? Or are they creating mental pressure, where you won't ever achieve what you're looking for?

❧

We are all works in progress. None of us is perfect, nor will we ever be. True respect is holding this space for others, seeing and loving them as they are, not how I want them to be. I wanted people to hold this same space for me and to see me as I was, as I was emerging. I needed to do the same for them.

Friendships changed as I set healthy boundaries, spoke my truth, minimized comparing and gossip, and recognized how I felt with certain people. As the unhealthy relationships went away, space opened, and more and more healthy, likeminded people appeared in my life.

Letting go of the old friendships was scary. I tend to do everything I can to make things work; however, that effort frequently went unrewarded. Eliminating those unhealthy friends made space, not just physically for new people to come in, but also emotionally. I was no longer energetically drained nor was my mind running in circles trying to figure out how to make something better.

Where do you need to let go? When you don't like something, you can always walk away. You do not have to get pulled into another person's madness. Remember that you can't save them. We all have our own journey to live.

৵৵

When we look objectively at the people who have come into our lives, we often see the state of mind we were in when we met them. And when we change and get healthier, our friendships and relationships tend to change and get healthier, too.

Chapter 9

The River Runs Wide

"*No legacy is so rich as honesty.*"
—William Shakespeare

By uncovering our families' legacies, learning more about why people made the decisions they did, and seeing how our environments impacted our decisions, we gain a level of understanding that can help us begin to let go of our past and move in healthier directions.

I am determined to see things differently. To let the past go, to let the stories go, to find forgiveness for the people in my life, I had to change the way I thought about them. I had to look beyond the specifics of the events and look at my part in the situations.

I had to look into my heart and this scared the heck out of me. I had been closed down for so long I wasn't sure how. Yet I continued the daily ACIM lessons and I began to let go. I saw myself begin to open and let down pieces of the old armor. I finally began to feel what I had held inside for so long.

One of the biggest lessons in ACIM is that the opposite of love isn't hate, it is fear. I was seeing how fear had driven so many of my decisions, even as simple as walking away because I was afraid of the unfamiliarity of someone or something. I was beginning to feel my heart and see why people had done the things they did.

As part of my third Al-Anon anniversary, I decided it was time to begin to pull the pieces together. I was seeing the legacy of alcoholism in my family, I was seeing how I had married what I was familiar with even though it was uncomfortable, and I was seeing my part in all of this.

It was time to speak my truth because I didn't want to hold it in anymore. I was ready to let go of the shame I had carried on my shoulders and in my heart for so many years. That Christmas, I had the opportunity to share my story with my mother. In those moments, my heart softened and I saw her in a different light. I saw that not only was she holding onto as much pain as I was, she also carried an incredible amount of guilt.

We don't know a lot about my father's side since he was adopted. There may or may not have been a history of alcoholism in his family. On my mother's side, however, it was like a second skin.

My grandmother and grandfather on my mom's side were both alcoholics. My grandfather was also a diabetic who died in his 50's due to the abuse on his body (one of my most vivid memories is of him putting a tab of butter on a hot ear of corn, letting it slide to the other end and then eating it with the corn, to be repeated multiple times per ear).

My grandmother wouldn't go to a restaurant that didn't serve liquor. Cocktails every day, which started earlier on the weekends. I saw more of this when I lived with her for those two summers and when she came to live with us. As a child, I didn't understand the hold that alcohol had on her. She was what I would call a functional alcoholic, who drank through dinner and evening TV and most nights fell asleep (passed out) on the couch. Functional was a safer label.

Both of my grandparents inherited the legacy of alcoholism. Although my grandfather was an angry man when at home, his friends loved him. He was happy with a cocktail in his hand.

My grandmother came from the same heritage. Her parents were difficult and unsupportive. She was married to Pop for

32 years, until his death. Where was she to go? She couldn't go back home, nor did she want to, based on the history in her familial household. There were fewer options then. So she stayed married to a man who was very difficult and ornery. I can't imagine spending 32 years with that man. Maybe she did love him, but my intuition tells me otherwise.

They had two children, my mother and my uncle Dick. I have heard some of the stories of growing up with Pop from my mother. From Dick, I will never know. He and his wife had four children and they moved to Texas to be nearer her family (or was it to get away from his?). I remember a visit from Dick when we lived in Sarasota. He did shots of vodka in the early morning, standing in our kitchen. He only stayed for a day or two.

We weren't close to that side of the family, and the next news I received was years later. Dick had stopped drinking under doctor's orders. Alcohol or death. He stopped for a few years, and then started again. Only he knows why. Our demons take hold just when we think we have them under control. He died in the bathroom of a gas station, on a trip bringing the kids home from camp. His stomach had burst. That is a legacy my cousins will live with forever. They were all in their teens or younger. Now without a father to guide them.

My mother grew up with a father and brother who mentally tormented her, and a mother who couldn't do a lot about it. My mother's heart issues started in her teens, and she too learned to not speak up.

The legacy of not feeling support from our mothers runs at least three generations, with each generation seemingly powerless to take on their respective situation. The impact of being raised by emotionally unavailable alcoholics deeply affected my mother. Not talking about feelings or what was happening in the family carries back to at least my great-grandparents.

The craziness carries from generation to generation, even if one of the generations doesn't drink. Many of the same, crazy characteristics are still taken on and expressed.

All four of Harry's siblings had substance abuse issues. His father as well as aunts and uncles were alcoholics. It ran on both sides of Dana's family. I was born into and married into it. It's no wonder I was so comfortable living with alcoholics.

I think back to the day at my grandparents' house, when my grandmother told me to ignore my grandfather's nastiness. She was essentially telling me how she had dealt with it all those years. When you can't protect yourself, how can you protect your children or grandchildren?

It doesn't excuse anything that happened in that house, yet it may help to explain why more wasn't done. What more could have been done? If you have no means and nowhere to go, you stay and make the best of it.

Sometimes to make peace, we sit on the barstool next to our spouse. We can't think of another way, so we go with what we know. What we grew up with and what's familiar. When it's familiar it doesn't feel odd. In what ways does this resonate with you?

❧

There are many reasons I chose not to have children. First, I go back to my childhood mantra. I was also terrified that I would somehow really screw up my kids. I didn't want my kids to be me. I didn't want to have that responsibility hanging over my head.

Then I married twice, in succession, to men who had young children who I adored, and I supported them the best way I could. I loved being able to pour my energy into the kids. It was easier with Harry's boys, who lived fifteen minutes away, than with Dana's girls who were five hours away.

In many ways I feel like I would have been an awesome mother, but I didn't trust myself enough. I didn't think I could do it the way I knew I wanted it done, and I didn't want to repeat what I grew up with. My instinct was spot on.

I know I made the right decision to not have children, yet there's a longing in my heart that remains open. As much as I think I secretly really wanted children, I knew in my heart that having a child with any of my significant exes was not the right thing to do. Maybe that's partly why I became so protective of my work teams, like they were my cubs. I fed them and sheltered them, and stood proud in their accomplishments.

My role in this life is to break the cycle of alcoholism. To break the cycle of abuse. To break the silence. To look deeply at the patterns in my family and my life, and uncover why people made the decisions they did. To find a deeper level of understanding.

I talked about breaking the cycle for years, yet I didn't look more deeply until I neared my third Al-Anon anniversary. I had examined the events that had happened in my life long enough. I was tired of repeating the same-old, same-old. I wanted to let it all go, and looking at the legacy gave me a new sense of compassion.

I was now able to understand some of the "why" behind the decisions in my family. Why my grandmother stayed with my grandfather. Why my mother fell in love with and married her second husband. Why she later remarried him after a divorce. Why we didn't share or show emotions. Why we didn't talk.

What are some of the recognizable patterns in your life? In your family? How often have you seen them repeated? List out both the good and the bad. There's often much good and happiness as well. In what ways have you followed in your family's footsteps?

Can you begin to see how the pieces fit together? Why did you make the decisions you did? How can you use that knowledge to let go of the old family stories? It's the stories we carry with us that define us—but only if we let them.

Chapter 10

Letting Go

*"Imagine you could open your eyes to see only the good
in every person, the positive in every circumstance,
and the opportunity in every challenge."*
—Rabbi M. M. Schneerson

T he decisions people make are rarely because of us. It is their own "stuff" that's driving them. Turning our attention toward what's our "stuff" and what's their "stuff" can clarify what we can't control and what we can.

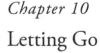

For many years I thought forgiveness meant that I had to be okay with a situation or with something a person had done.

There were countless things that I wasn't okay with, so I didn't let them go. Two things started to change my perspective *acceptance doesn't mean agreement* and *forgiveness is for us.* By accepting the situations I didn't like, I was able to let them go and thus release the energy associated with them. I could forgive a situation and thus release myself of the burden.

In that sense, forgiveness was totally for me. If I was stewing about a situation and the other person had no idea, what good did it do for me to hold onto it? They were going about their life, with the situation probably long forgotten. Holding onto it wasn't doing me a bit of good. Yet letting go wasn't always easy.

Think of some of your old situations you're not happy about. What do you need to do to let it go? Is the person still in your life? If not, why do you let it still bother you? If so, can you talk with them? Or write them a letter? The letter doesn't even need to be sent, the purpose is to get out on paper all of your thoughts and emotions, so they no longer run through your mind.

∻

Forgiveness also came from looking at the situations of my past and understanding "can't do" vs. "won't do." I began to understand that for the people in my life, it often wasn't a matter of them not wanting to do something, they weren't able to emotionally. Case in point the old man down the street.

My mother was newly divorced with three young children, working full time: she had her hands full. Back then, things like that weren't talked about. I realized that I put a current day perspective on an old event, which caused me more heartache. Walking around feeling wounded only surrounded me with negative energy.

Think back to the stressful situations in your life. Does the "can't do" vs. "won't do" argument apply for any of them? Are you able to put a lens on how the person acted based on that timeframe, not with a current lens? Does it change your perspective? Does it soften how you feel about the situation?

∻⸙

If you can approach a situation or conversation with another person with the thought that the other person is approaching with a positive intent, it creates a space free of negativity. There are some people who aren't kind, yet the majority of people are trying to do the right thing, from their perspective.

Can you think of a current situation and change your perspective by putting on a lens of positive intent? How does this change your thoughts about your part as well as the other person's? Letting go of the negative "what if" frees your energy to focus on more positive solutions.

∻⸙

When I look back at some of my family situations, I realize that many decisions were made out of fear. My grandmother couldn't go back home and thus had nowhere else to go. My mother always wanted a family, and my father was rarely home. She remarried her second husband because she didn't have the means to financially support us on her own.

When you feel like you don't have control, fear kicks in and you make decisions based on damage control. Although the decisions that people around us make sometimes affect us, they are rarely made because of us. Thinking there is some kind of conspiracy against you keeps you in victim mode and doesn't allow you to let go of the old energy.

Life is hard and messy and sometimes you screw up. Sometimes there's an opportunity to make amends. My grandmother did this with me. She doted on me and protected me as best she could because she wasn't able to do so for my mother. My mother wanted the same opportunity to do this with my children that, ultimately, weren't to be.

When you grow up, you realize there are some things in your past that you'd do differently, given the chance. But you can't change the past, and continuing to focus on the old stories keeps you small. Don't you get tired of repeating the same old patterns? I certainly did. I realized how toxic it was to my body and my mind.

Letting go is a gradual process. Once I had released something, often something else would come up that I didn't even realize I was holding onto. I couldn't let go of everything all at once.

I also had to look back and remember that not everything sucked. There were many good times as well. Running around the neighborhood, climbing trees, riding bikes, ice skating. Remembering the good provides balance. None of it can be changed, good or bad. If some of your situations go back to your childhood, what are the good things you remember? Who stands out, be it friends or family who stood by you?

Now think about the situations, past and future, that run through your mind on a regular basis. How much time are they taking away from what you could be focusing on right now? How much space is cleared when you remove thoughts about the past and future? How much more can you get done on what you have directly in front of you now, and how much more quickly?

❧❧

Eckhart Tolle, coming from his own personal breakdown, has written an amazing book called *The Power of Now*. In it, he argues that we cannot change the past, nor can we predict the future: instead, we should focus on mindfulness and being in the present moment. If you think about it, tomorrow will never exist.

You can make the most of the present moment that you're in. To me, that was incredibly freeing. I can do the best I can, right now, and then move on to the next moment.

Worrying about tomorrow takes my focus off of *now*. Lamenting about the past does the same. Realizing this gave me a very different perspective on how I approach my thoughts and letting go. I could think of 100 ways a situation might turn out, and rarely did one of them happen. Think of all the time we waste thinking about something that was never to be.

෨෨

A tool I continue to use to this day is journaling. Being able to put my thoughts into words has been cathartic. There are days when my writing focus is on something bothering me. Other days on an idea, or a connection I've made about something. Or I will write a letter that will never be sent.

For many years I didn't have a journal for fear of someone reading it. I didn't want anyone to know my thoughts, so I kept them inside. By getting those thoughts out on paper, they lost some of their hold over me and I found that my thoughts became clearer. I write when the mood strikes.

I do have one ceremony I perform every year on New Years Day and that is to burn the prior year's journals. To me, watching the paper go up in flames releases the energy that went into the pages. I call it a "good burn," and it's quite cathartic. There have been times I will do this with a singular letter. To put my thoughts and emotions on paper and then watch it turn to ashes can be quite satisfying.

Who do you need to write a letter to that won't be sent, but will instead be burned? Can you see how having a journal to get the thoughts out of your head can lead to letting them go all together? And how doing this can begin to clear the energy between you and the other person?

∂∞∂

Clearing the energy, even if it's one-sided, is crucial to letting go and forgiveness. The other person may hold onto their side of the story for a long time, but that's none of your business. You can only change how you feel. Don't you want to feel better?

Which brings me back to the ACIM lesson about how everything has the meaning we give to it. You can make something as big or as small in your mind as you want.

Around the same time I found ACIM, I learned of a book titled *Zero Limits*, in which the old Hawaiian practice of Ho'oponopono is presented in a more modern form. The practice originated as one of forgiveness and reconciliation, and was used to repair families.

Zero Limits shares a new perspective on this tradition where people take full responsibility for their lives. By repeatedly saying the mantra of "I love you. I'm sorry. Please forgive me. Thank you," you are working to clear the energy between yourself and the person to whom you're saying the prayer.

It goes much deeper, as does ACIM and *The Power of Now*. Yet all three bring together the combined ideas of forgiving and letting go of the past, focusing on the present moment, and giving as much or as little significance to things as we want. Combined, these are incredible tools to use for letting go.

But first you have to make the decision to *want* to forgive and to let go of the old stories you've carried for so many years. Are you ready to take 100% responsibility for your life? For your relationships and how you think about and approach them? Are you ready to let go?

కాల

When we hold onto our old stories, they hold us back both mentally and physically. We do not have to *agree* with the events of our past, but *accepting* them can free us and can begin to bring us to a place of forgiveness.

Chapter 11

Coming Home

"There is grace for every soul."
—Lailah Gifty Akita

F inding compassion for yourself, as you find it for others, is paramount to your recovery, because we are often the hardest on ourselves. Being on an even plane with others in our lives relieves us of the distorted expectations we have for ourselves.

❧

Accepting old situations and finding forgiveness for myself was something that came harder for me. It was so easy to beat myself up for the decisions I made, the things I did to my body. The shame of staying in situations as long as I did in the effort to try to make them work, even though they weren't good for me. Not standing up for myself in toxic situations. The list was long.

I had to let go of the resentments I felt toward my ex-husbands. I was a part of both of those relationships, and I had put on blinders. With Harry, I found out after we had split where a lot of the money was going. I had questioned, but I don't think I really wanted to know at the time. When I found out I was shocked, yet it made so much sense and it tied everything together. The same with Dana, yet I knew when we were still together, but only after he went to rehab. To beat myself up over this does me no good now. They're pieces of the puzzle, answers that I can acknowledge and now put away.

What are some of the old resentments that you can think of to release, where you ignored or pretended to not know what was happening in order to protect yourself?

ॐॐ

I had felt abandoned for so many years, when in reality I had abandoned myself. I participated in my life; however, it was like I was free floating through it. I had given away my power in search of happiness. Looking for that happiness and fulfillment outside of myself rather than doing what I needed to feed my soul.

Are there ways you've not stood up for yourself? Ways in which you've looked for things outside of yourself for happiness and fulfillment? Awareness is the first step.

❧❦

Finding forgiveness for myself meant letting go of the guilt and the shame. Brené Brown has a beautiful definition for these: "Guilt says I did something bad, shame says I am bad."

I wasn't always kind to members of my family, especially my mother. I placed much of the blame on her, and did my very best to make her feel as much pain as I was feeling.

It was convenient to point the finger at her. Yet I had rejected her guidance starting in high school and didn't make life easy on either of us.

I am not proud of some of the things I did. Nevertheless, I need to have the same level of compassion for myself as I do others. I was doing the best I could with what I had. I was never going to feel like I had roots until I came home to myself.

Where do you need to let go of guilt for things you did that you're not proud of? Where do you need to let go of shame for things where you labeled yourself as bad and took on something that wasn't yours to take?

Guilt is a useless emotion that keeps us in our place.

❧❦

I found comfort in the old stories, until I didn't anymore. It took major events for me to finally decide that I wanted something better for myself. I wanted to feel differently and to do so I had to let go of the old stories and my old limiting beliefs I had told myself for so many years. I had to let go of the things that were never mine to take in the first place and to be totally responsible for myself. To stand in my own power and my own future.

What limiting beliefs do you carry with you that hold you back? Are they really true, or do they date back to the old stories that you've carried with you for far too long?

∂∘∾

I don't know how many years I have left on this earth, but I've made the decision that I want to live them in the best possible way. When I started to remove the negative from my life, I began to recognize how much abundance I have around me.

Abundance to me is about seeing the beauty in everything around me, close friendships, laughter, music, art, good food. Making the choice every day to do things to feel the way I want to feel. Making the choice to speak my truth and say what I need.

Being in healthy relationships and setting healthy boundaries are two of the best ways I can respect myself. I am surrounded more and more by healthy, like-minded people.

People who are happy, who see the abundance all around them and who find the joy amidst the challenges.

By saying what I want and don't want, I am standing up for myself. It gives people parameters to work with. If my boundaries aren't okay with a person, then do I really want them in my life anyway?

I lived for so many years without boundaries. I let people walk all over me in certain relationships. I now recognize this and set new standards as I move forward.

What boundaries can you establish for yourself today, to begin to stand up more for yourself? Can you identify the joy in your life, amidst the challenges you're facing? Before you go to sleep tonight, can you say thanks for at least one thing you're grateful for, reflecting on where you find abundance in your life?

❧

I am a work in progress and so are you. Remember to have compassion for yourself. This can be hard sometimes. It was for me. I judged myself for years, quite harshly sometimes.

We're all human and make mistakes. It is up to us to learn from them, brush ourselves off, let them go and then move forward. That's how you learn and grow. Perfection doesn't exist.

Where can you let go of judgment and perfection?

❧

I can remember that "No" is a one-word answer, and that I don't have to always feel the need to explain myself. I used to feel like I had to explain all of my decisions, to somehow justify them to other people. Words that were rarely heard.

Standing tall with the decisions I make now is a way of respecting myself. I don't have to explain. Saying "No" can be quite empowering.

Where are you doing things that you don't want to do, where you can bow out and say "No" to create time and space for yourself?

❧

Now I'm making peace with my past, and remembering that acceptance doesn't mean agreement. I did the best I could with what I had. If I hadn't been through all of these experiences, I wouldn't be where I am today.

The future looks amazing. There will be challenges. I will make mistakes. I will feel heartache and loss. Yet I am approaching life now from a perspective of positive intent and abundance. There is enough for all of us.

Are there places in your life where you can find acceptance for your part of your story? To let go of comparison and judgment? To come to a place of peace, knowing that you are exactly where you're supposed to be? To recognize the lesson before you?

❧❦

You have a choice to continue to live as you are, or to move forward into your future, free of your past. You can show yourself the same level of compassion that you show others. You can make the decision to feel differently.

You can remember that you are doing the best you can with what you have and that you made decisions you thought were right at the time you made them. You can use the same lens on yourself that you use with other people. Are you ready?

My intuition is a great guide for me now. By clearing the mental and energetic clutter, I've created space for connection and inspiration. I've created space to hold for others. I've come to a place where I really like who I am.

❧❦

When we continue to point the finger at ourselves, it keeps us in an old, small space. Love yourself as you love others.

Conclusion

"You raze the old to raise the new."
—Justina Chen

There is a lesson in everything we do and in everything that happens to us. The beauty is in being willing to learn that lesson. I shared my story with you in the hopes that you may learn from it and begin to find hope and peace in your own life. That your journey be faster based on leveraging the lessons of mine.

The challenges of our family legacies and the legacy we make within our own life doesn't have to define us. Our families shape our identity; yet we are not our stories. There is so much of what we live with that is passed from generation to generation.

By looking at the past, you can see how the pieces fit together and what drove you to where you are now. How building walls and letting fear control your decisions ultimately gives away your power.

I don't want you to suffer in silence. I want you to become true to yourself and find your voice, to let go of what you've held on to for so long. To no longer bury your thoughts and feelings within your body and to find a healthy outlet for them. My wish for you is that you uncover the greatness of who you are meant to be, despite the chaos of living with an alcoholic.

Take a few minutes to think about why you read this book. How will you take its lessons forward in your life? My hope is you embrace the lessons and utilize the tools that resonate with you. Our journey of letting go is an iterative process and one that can be both surprising and liberating.

One of the things that can keep you on track is to find an accountability partner. I walked through much of my life feeling very alone, and now thrive in connection, community and sharing.

Many times the reason people stop their self-exploration is out of fear, and those of us living with an alcoholic often have a greater level of fear. My wish for you is that you step onto a new path, one where you leave the fear behind and approach life from a new perspective. You can be free.

Autobiography in
Five Short Chapters
By Portia Nelson

I.

I walk down the street.

There is a deep hole in the sidewalk.

I fall in.

I am lost…

I am hopeless.

It isn't my fault.

It takes me forever to find a way out.

II.

I walk down the same street.

There is a deep hole in the sidewalk.

I pretend I don't see it.

I fall in again.

I can't believe I am in the same place.
But, it isn't my fault.
It still takes a long time to get out.

III.

I walk down the same street.
There is a deep hole in the sidewalk.
I see it is there.
I still fall in… it's a habit.
My eyes are open.
I know where I am.
It is my fault.
I get out immediately.

IV.

I walk down the same street.
There is a deep hole in the sidewalk.
I walk around it.

V.

I walk down another street.

Further Reading

The 100 Day Promise, by Sandi Amorim
The Power of Now, by Eckhart Tolle
Men, Women & Worthiness, by Brené Brown
The Desire Map, by Danielle LaPorte
Zero Limits, by Joe Vitale
A Course in Miracles, by Dr. Helen Schucman
No More F***ing Secrets, by Jill Prescott
Long Ago Elf, by Mary and R.A. Smith

Acknowledgments

There are so many people who have supported me on my journey.

Thanks to my mother and father for having me, so that I could walk through this journey.

Thanks to Sandi Amorim. Through my work with her, I was given a safe space to begin to discover myself and learn how I wanted to feel.

Thanks to Jill Prescott, for providing a safe space for me to explore the energy behind the ties to my old stories, and to work through them at my own pace.

Thanks to the Revivalists, for the amazing music they create. Their music helped me through the transition of my divorce and of me finding myself. Music speaks to me on many levels, and theirs reaches my soul.

Thanks to the RevHeads, the amazing fan group of the Revivalists. With them I found connection. We have a unified love of the music and seeing y'all at shows brings much joy and allows my inner child out to play.

Thanks to my fellow Al-Anon brothers and sisters. With them I found my voice and they accepted me with love and without judgment.

Thanks to my Idea to Done cohort, led by the amazing Angela Lauria. Week by week we worked through and faced our fears to write a book that could make a difference. Being of service is my utmost goal, and they made sure we didn't fall off the rails.

To the Morgan James Publishing team: Special thanks to David Hancock, CEO & Founder for believing in me and my message. To my Author Relations Manager, Margo Toulouse thanks for making the process seamless and easy. Many more thanks to everyone else, but especially Jim Howard, Bethany Marshall, and Nickcole Watkins.

Thanks to everyone else who has graced my life, as I wouldn't be where I am today if it weren't for them.

About the Author

Stephanie McAuliffe is a truth-seeker and personal archaeologist. Just before Hurricane Sandy, her world was turned upside down when her husband entered rehab for alcoholism.

She knows firsthand what life is like living with the chaos of this disease and how deeply it affects families, often many generations back. She uses her expertise in identifying and putting together the pieces of the puzzle to understand our intricate ties. Our families shape our identity, yet we are not our stories.

She believes there is power in giving a voice to our stories and more importantly in understanding the "why" behind them. She believes there should be no shame in giving them a voice and is living proof that in voicing them we can finally let them go.

Stephanie is guided by her values of honesty, integrity, truth and love. Her path now leads her to one of being of service. She seeks to help people uncover and tell their truth, and to connect on a different level. She is a living example that we can heal and clear the energy passed from prior generations, break the cycle, and in the process uncover the greatness of who we are meant to be.

Stephanie is an avid organic gardener and live music lover who lives on the Jersey Shore.

Website: www.stephaniebmcauliffe.com
Email: stephaniebmcauliffe@gmail.com

Thank You

Thank you so much for sharing this journey, and trusting me to guide you. The fact that you've gotten to this point in the book tells me something important about you: you're ready. You're ready to shift out of the chaos. You're ready to bring hope and peace into your days. Most importantly, you're ready to free your mind of the old stories and the things you can't control. This isn't the end, but rather the beginning.

To help you identify which of the aspects covered in this book may be affecting you in your life, I've created the Your Message Assessment. It's a simple diagnostic tool to help you home in on where you may want to initially direct your focus.

To access the assessment, simply go to
www.themessageinthebottlebook.com/bonus.

Morgan James
Speakers Group

www.TheMorganJamesSpeakersGroup.com

We connect Morgan James published
authors with live and online events
and audiences who will benefit
from their expertise.

Printed in the USA
CPSIA information can be obtained
at www.ICGtesting.com
JSHW082353140824
68134JS00020B/2066